THE LANGUAGE OF DRAWINGS

THE LANGUAGE
OF DRAWINGS

A New Finding in
Psychodynamic Work

A. H. Brafman

KARNAC

First published in 2012 by
Karnac Books Ltd
118 Finchley Road, London NW3 5HT

British Library Cataloguing in Publication Data

A C.I.P. for this book is available from the British Library

ISBN 978 1 78049 017 5

Edited, designed and produced by The Studio Publishing Services Ltd
www.publishingservicesuk.co.uk
e-mail: studio@publishingservicesuk.co.uk

Printed in Great Britain

www.karnacbooks.com

CONTENTS

To Lilian, a constant source of valuable support

ACKNOWLEDGEMENTS

I am grateful to all the children and families who enabled me to produce this book.

My special thanks to Rosine Perelberg for her inspirational advice.

Dr A. H. Brafman worked as a consultant child and adolescent psychiatrist in the National Health Service until his retirement. He is a qualified psychoanalyst of adults and children, and gave seminars on infant observation for trainees of the British Psychoanalytic Society and other training institutions. For many years, he ran a weekly meeting for under-fives and their parents at Queen Mary's Hospital, Roehampton, London. He has published four books based on his work with children and parents: *Untying the Knot* (Karnac, 2001); *Can You Help Me?* (Karnac, 2004); *The 5–10-Year-Old Child* (Karnac, 2010); *Fostering Independence* (Karnac, 2011), as well as a series of papers on various clinical topics. For several years, under the sponsorship of the Winnicott Trust, he ran weekly clinical seminars for medical students at the University Hospital Medical School, Department of Psychotherapy.

Introduction

A lady referred her sixteen-year-old stepson for a consultation. She had brought him up from the age of seven, when she married his father, after his mother had left the family three years earlier. He was now presenting problems at school and he had become obsessed with visiting a couple who ran a youth group. In the course of our interview, he drew a picture of the wife of this couple sitting sideways on a chair and went on to draw several other images. As our conversation progressed, he turned the page over and drew an altar. I thought it puzzling that he had drawn this image with lighter lines, not so clearly defined as those on the first page. I picked up the paper and, as I was indicating my interest in his choice of subject, I noticed that the lady was now lying over the altar (see Alan, pp. 74–78). When I showed him this superimposition, he was surprised and somewhat embarrassed; he could recognise how, from an unconscious point of view, this lady had come to fill the gap left by his mother, who had abandoned the family when he was four years old.

To my surprise, I later found other examples of drawings where an emotionally significant image had been split into two and displayed in separate, sequential pictures that, in isolation, would not allow one to recognise their unconscious meaning. It is this phenomenon of split drawings that is the subject of this book. This is a fascinating and puzzling form of communication, whereby a person allows us to find the cues to understand thoughts and feelings that underlie the problems that bring him to consult us.

According to the *Oxford English Dictionary*, "communication" is defined as "the imparting or exchanging of information by speaking, writing, or using some other medium". Considering this definition, we should recognise two implications: one is that the subject actually intends to convey some message to the other, and two, the other needs to be prepared to consider the subject's message carefully, so as to understand what he actually wants to express.

There are times when the other purports to understand what the subject is conveying and we find the subject denying that he ever intended to transmit any such message. A common example of this type of doubtful "communication" is those situations when a person sighs or swears and finds himself bombarded with expressions of sympathy or irritation from someone near him. When it is normal adults that are involved, there is no serious trouble in such misunderstandings, since further discussion can clarify any doubts or mistakes. We have a more complex situation when the two people do not speak the same language or have any kind of impediment that requires the use of other means of communication than ordinary language, as is the case, for example, when addressing someone who is deaf. When a young person is involved, we also find a multitude of difficult and subtle problems: age, command of language, and level of cognitive development introduce limits to the possibility of sorting out any apparent doubts or misunderstandings and the context of the meeting is equally important, since the child or adolescent might not feel totally free to express his views.

When a baby cries, is this a communication or merely the expression of some physical discomfort or distress? Whatever an outsider might argue, the baby's carers will respond as if receiving a plea from the baby; that is, the crying is interpreted as a message, where the baby is seen to be trying to convey a particular thought or feeling. Many mothers claim that they can distinguish between the baby's crying when hungry and his crying when in pain, but the vital test in such situations is the mother's capacity to "try again" with some different interpretation when the crying persists. If the mother reacts with feelings of anxiety, panic, or despair, the chances are that the baby will now also react to her emotional distress, with the strong possibility of a pattern being set up where child and mother repeatedly trigger these anxiety-driven reactions in each other (Brafman, 2004, p. 5).

Watching a newborn developing over his early weeks and months, we can distinguish a subtle process of adaptation between baby and parents, where significant patterns are developed. As the infant grows older, this process of development comes to include those innumerable elements that characterise the ethos of the baby's world. Not only will he speak his parents' language, but he will also have internalised (adopted as his own) styles of behaviour that will distinguish him from his peers. Toilet training, feeding habits, the manner of addressing siblings and older people, styles of dressing—there is no end to what comes to characterise that individual child as being a member of his family. The obvious, but still fascinating, point is that when we approach a particular child or adolescent, it might be virtually impossible to differentiate what, in his presentation, is part of his inborn endowment and what is the result of his adaptation to his early environment.

Many studies have identified the parameters that enable us to assess the development of a child's cognitive ability and, thereby, discover when a child requires an educational or therapeutic input to remedy some shortcoming or impediment. These tests study the child's capacity to understand the world he lives in and also his skills in utilising this input in order to express his thoughts, feelings, needs, and wishes. Living close to a young, developing child is an exciting and fascinating experience, since we can savour each new step to full verbal articulacy. From unrecognisable sounds to repeated ones addressed to a particular person, leading eventually to that pronunciation that represents the appellation for that individual, we see the child enjoying the response to his vocal efforts that are always accompanied by facial expressions and movements of the head and/or hands. It is this global image that allows parents to grasp not only who is being addressed, but also the child's emotional experience at that particular moment. Obviously, the older the child gets, the more he comes to rely on words to convey his thoughts and feelings, but it is part of normal development that each child will resort to various other means to express himself when unable to articulate his intended communications.

Some children will cry, others will make unusual movements with various parts of the body, others will pick up different toys before or while speaking, others will suddenly move clumsily and stumble: there is no end of variations, but what is so noteworthy is the subtle way in which the child learns what is and what is not understood by each parent and by other people in his world and proceeds to absorb and utilise this in line with his feelings and intentions at that particular moment. A simple example of this world-adaptive learning can be seen in children whose parents come from different countries and/or speak different languages: most children will learn to speak these different languages to each parent, and then, when wanting to antagonise them, will speak the "wrong" language to one of the parents.

It is the response the child receives from the parents that gradually builds what Freud (1923b) called the "ego" and the "super-ego". The ego corresponds to what we might call the "self", those functions of the personality that characterise the person's image of himself and of those in his world. The superego is the section of the mind that registers the criticisms, injunctions, demands, all the features that constitute the ethical standards of the child's family and the society in which they live. In practice, the superego represents the unconscious record of what is not approved by the parents and that can lead the child to a situation of trouble if put into practice. Especially when considering an older child, we speak of his learning to display "good behaviour". We do not consider the child insincere or hypocritical, but we can recognise that there is a process of self-censorship where spontaneity seems to decrease or disappear. Winnicott (1960) came to describe what he called a "false self", the result of a process of adaptation to the personality of one or both parents. But it is very important to note that if there is historical justification for the child to develop such a façade towards that parent, it is rather surprising to find that child adopting the same process of self-censure when dealing with most or all other people. It must be stressed that this is an unconscious process, definitely not the same as the child *deciding* to keep something secret from the world.

This process of adaptation of the child to the world in which he lives must be borne in mind when we meet a child for the first time. Depending on his age and his basic personality, he will respond to our approach in line with those developmental patterns. Indeed, our gender, our age, and our approach will influence his response, but the child has to contend with his private conscious and unconscious ideas of how to deal with someone he has not met before. It is this complex network of features that has led psychoanalysts to postulate a range of "mechanisms" to explain the emotional experience of the child. He will perceive the stranger in line with the *projection* of his *internal objects* that are stirred up in his conscious and unconscious mind. These internal objects are the result of his *internalisation* of features of his close objects and subsequent elaboration of these images because of the feelings aroused in the child by further interactions with these objects. As the child focuses attention on what he was told or asked to do, his potential reaction meets a number of memories resulting from his previous experiences and, if these arouse feelings that might lead to trauma or conflict, then *resistances* and *unconscious defences* come into operation and he will only articulate those words or embark on actions that he believes will not trigger off a repetition of those earlier traumatic experiences (see Laplanche & Pontalis, 1973).

Awareness of these patterns that characterise the child's daily interactions with his world is very important when the child shows signs of distress. It happens, all too often, that the child does not know the precise reason for his distress, and will then get hold of any complaint that he has learnt will mobilise his parents' attention. All parents are only too familiar with these recurring complaints and with the difficulty of obtaining from the child a clear explanation of what is upsetting him. Unfortunately, many parents do not manage to accept the explanation that some of these children do not truly know what makes them anxious, and that we also find children who will not articulate their thoughts when they fear such words might upset the parents. This is an added difficulty when one tries to understand and perhaps comfort and help the child.

Careful observation of the child's behaviour will help us pick up signs that can lead us to explore what thoughts and feelings the child is experiencing and struggling with. The child who suddenly one day refuses to sit on the toilet is probably reacting to an underlying image of the toilet as dangerous. Quite often, children will claim an "upset tummy" that prevents them from going to school when, in fact, they are struggling with fears of attending classes. The child's refusal to fall asleep is probably a pointer to the presence of nightmares. The child's play with his toys will often contain a representation of his experiences, which points to the importance of paying attention to the details of his play. When the child begins to pick up pen or pencil and draws, it is well worth trying to learn what exactly is being depicted.

But these are not new findings. Children have puzzled adults since time immemorial, and recognising significant behaviours that might throw light on the child's conscious and unconscious experience of life is particularly important when the child is unhappy, anxious, or distressed. It is not surprising that children's drawings became a crucial element in the exploration of the child's experience of life, since they did not seem to mobilise in the child those conscious and unconscious conflicts related to his feelings of what was "right" to express or, conversely, dangerous or improper.

Studies of children's drawings have been carried out for centuries. Focusing on their contents, the challenge lay in correlating what was on paper with what supposedly might be their representation in words. Stern (1924) pointedly depicted this parallel by arguing that the initial scribbles relate to drawing as babbling does to speech. Indeed, the child's drawing abilities go through a process of maturation and, over the years, many authors have put forward parameters to gauge the stage of development reached by the child in his representation of self and others. This means that, much as happens with spoken language, irrespective of considering artistic potential, children's drawings are a precious datum in helping us to learn of their thoughts, feelings, desires, pains, dreams, etc.

Furthermore, it was found that whatever the cultural environment in which the children are growing up, when they use pen or pencil to represent a human figure, the drawings made by children of the same age show a series of common patterns (Kellogg, 1969). Eventually, it was recognised that the child's life experiences influenced certain features of their drawings, and this led authors to investigate those characteristics that might help in the recognition of possible psychological or neurological pathology. Children's drawings were now seen as a valid expression of the child's emotional experience of himself and of the world around him. Classical examples of these studies can be found in Piaget and Inhelder (1967), Luquet (2001), and Lowenfeld (1947).

Repeating what was said above, what is at stake is the search for a valid route to assess the ideation of a child, once it is acknowledged that the child's capacity to communicate his thoughts and feelings is restricted by his cognitive development and/or by a multitude of unconscious factors that prevent their expression. In fact, adolescents and adults will also resort to this unconscious mechanism of self-protection when they repress elements of a situation that they experienced as painful and traumatic. Again, the trauma will produce its physical and/or emotional impact but the person involved might find it difficult to identify the precise reason why the experience was so hurtful and damaging.

Trying to explore a person's report of a traumatic experience, we find that, however unable to provide a full, detailed account of events, the person (whatever their age) has a definite image of what happened and this can be found in his words or in drawings. Discussing this relationship between perception, memory, and the expression of thoughts through drawings, Arnheim (1969, p. 97) quotes Zuccari, who already, in 1607, referred to *disegno interno* and *disegno esterno*, to underline how the memories of our life experiences are stored as *images*, but these images are not photographic, objective reproductions of the actual events as visually perceived. They are, rather, the result of distortions produced by emotional impulses experienced at the time of the original event.

Psychological studies of large numbers of children have led to the identification of features in their drawings that indicate particular emotional configurations. Di Leo (1973) is one of these authors, and perhaps one example will illustrate this approach to children's drawings:

> The absence of arms in drawings by children over six may be indicative of timidity, passivity or intellectual immaturity. The omission becomes most unusual by age ten, when over 90 percent will draw the arms. . . . Vane and Eisen include omission of arms as one of four signs which identify a high percentage of maladjusted children between 5 years 3 months and 6 years 5 months of age. The other three indicators were found to be absence of body, absence of mouth and grotesque figure. Hidden hands have been interpreted as an expression of guilt feelings. (p. 38)

These studies of children of all ages have aimed at establishing statistically valid configurations that pinpoint how the child experienced particular events, situations, or relationships. We find works focusing on abuse, disabling conditions, and traumatic experiences, among other subjects. A detailed survey of this literature can be found in Moore (1994). Considering the focus of the present text, we should note her reference to Johnson's (1985) statement that "we hold memories in separate and not always verbally accessible parts of our mind". It is interesting to consider how this neuropsychological formulation gives a physical substratum to the psychoanalytic concept that some memories are retained in an unconscious part of the mind because of emotional resistances and defences.

While the psychological approach focuses on statistically significant findings and techniques that might help the worker to appraise the problems of the individual patient, the psychodynamic professional aims at approaching the patient with no preconceptions. Indeed, this is an ideal, since information gathered from whoever referred the patient will influence one's views, much as all the impressions one forms when actually meeting the person. Nevertheless, the objective is to elicit information that will enable the clinician to understand the particular individual now under his care. Depending on this client's age, the professional will have to resort to various "languages" through which that person will convey his conscious and unconscious thoughts and feelings. Words, vocal intonations, facial expressions, body movements, the mode of relating to the clinician, these are all data that lead the psychodynamic worker to formulate the questions that might enable the patient to express his feelings in words. Children, however, pose a special challenge because of the characteristics of their emotional development that were mentioned above. Not surprisingly, we often find similar difficulties when seeing an adolescent. When we reach the point where it is clear that the child or adolescent will not manage to put all his thoughts and feelings into words, it becomes necessary to explore alternative means of communication.

Psychoanalysts had been applying their theories to the treatment of emotionally disturbed adults for some two decades before some brave practitioners decided to explore their applicability to helping children in distress. Hug-Hellmuth, Anna Freud, and Klein were the pioneers in this new field of work. They soon found that, contrary to their practice with adults, more than a verbal exchange was required to gain knowledge of the child's conflicts. Presumably because of their previous experience of working and living with children, they made play materials available, and the child could use these to construct shapes, draw pictures, and make up stories. But they put forward different evaluations of the child's productions. Klein (1932) saw "play" as virtually synonymous with spoken language and approached it within the same theoretical framework that she had formulated to explain the psychoanalytic interaction with adult patients. Anna Freud (1927), by contrast, stressed that when using this approach it was vital to take into account the distortions that the analyst might make when interpreting the non-verbal play of the child. She saw play as valuable, but only as one of the elements that had to be taken into account when trying to understand the interaction between child and analyst.

It was Winnicott (1971) who brought drawings to the front line of analytic work with children. A senior paediatrician, he was also a gifted (graphic and musical) artist. Working in his child psychiatric clinic, he discovered that, however shy or reserved children were when approached in spoken language, they were easily able to engage in making pictures. He would propose to the child they should play a game of squiggles, proceeding to make such a squiggle and asking the child to make something out of it; once finished, the child would make his own squiggle that Winnicott turned into a picture. After a series of such drawings, Winnicott was able to discern the unconscious conflicts underlying the child's symptoms.

A child (or a patient of any age) will only come to consult a psychoanalyst, or any professional, when experiencing problems that interfere with their usual, normal life. The professional has to conduct a diagnostic assessment of his patient in order to establish the nature of his problems and the best way in which to bring relief of his symptoms. Some children's symptoms might be caused by cognitive and/or emotional abnormalities, and these will require complex educational and remedial long-term input. But the majority of children and adolescents seen by a psychoanalyst present reactions to situations or relationships experienced as traumatic, and these are difficulties that usually respond to a limited therapeutic intervention.

In most cases, we find that a person experiences an actual, conscious event as traumatic because it triggers off a link with a past situation that has been "stored" in the person's unconscious. Seeing the patient, we hear his recollection (i.e., his version, his interpretation) of the recent traumatic event and we set out to explore the presumed unconscious memory of an earlier traumatic event (Perelberg, 2007). Interviewing an adolescent or adult, the consultant will watch for slips of the tongue, enquire about dreams, listen to the patient's account of his daily present and past experiences, and consider how the patient is relating to him, seeing all of these as cues that will point to the nature of the underlying unconscious experience that might then explain why the patient reacted to his recent traumatic life situation in the manner he demonstrated and described.

When we see a child in the consulting room, it is important to make available toys, games, paper, and drawing materials, the use of which will help us understand the child's conflicts. There is no question that the child's behaviour when in front of the analyst is ever a refusal to make contact. A silent child who sits with his back to the analyst is probably indicating his belief that the analyst will not want, or not be able, to help him. It is a fundamental assumption that we must treat the child's behaviour, words, and play as his attempts to communicate to us the content of his thoughts and feelings. This is a child or adolescent experiencing pain, anxiety, discomfort, or unhappiness, and he knows that seeing a professional represents the hope that he will find help and relief: it is obvious that he will try to express his feelings, but each child or adolescent will do this in his own way. One hopes that the professional will succeed in gaining the child's confidence.

After an initial contact, where the consultant tries to make the child feel comfortable, most children will accept answering questions about their life and experiences. Once the professional has a reasonably clear view of the child's view of himself and his world, it is useful to suggest that the child makes some drawing. He will always ask, "Draw what?" and it is best to suggest he draws whatever he wants. Having looked at this drawing and heard the child's description of it, one suggests that he draws another picture. These two or more drawings and the accompanying comments help the clinician to decide what questions or comments to make in order to reach an understanding of the child's reaction to his traumatic experience.

As described above, the child's drawings do not seem to be subject to the same unconscious mechanisms that govern the child's speech. The child or adolescent will be able to draw a traumatic situation "as it happened", but very often this will not depict his actual unconscious experience. However, we can find that, much as happens with words, the person will split his thoughts and feelings and express them as if not related, this being an unconscious self-protective defence to avoid further pain. Each drawing represents the conscious image the child has of the present or past actual or imaginary theme he depicts, and the clinician's challenge is to consider these pictures and words so as to understand the unconscious emotional conflict underlying the child's reaction to the traumatic experience. It is important to appreciate that when these split verbal or graphic messages are expressed to a professional, one must conclude that they come to the surface due to an underlying hope that help will be offered and relief finally experienced.

This book presents a series of clinical interviews where children and adolescents made drawings displaying split images, and this is a phenomenon that seems not to have been previously described in the literature. These were drawings made separately, but when seen superimposed on each other, as if constituting a single picture, they revealed a specific meaning that would not be recognised if considering the pictures individually. Looking at this "reconstituted" image, every single child and adolescent reacted with words of surprise and recognition.

At one point, I also found this same phenomenon of split images in drawings made by art college students in an experimental setting and some of these are shown here, but most of the cases to be presented come from work with children and adolescents in a clinical setting.

Split images

Bridget

The general practitioner referred Bridget, aged twelve, because her mother had found that Bridget had stolen some money from her purse and that she had also been truanting from school. Mrs B was immensely distraught and crying when she spoke to the secretary to make the appointment. She felt that suddenly some colossal gap had opened up between Bridget and herself; she described asking Bridget questions and meeting no more than "a vacant look". Mrs B wanted to see the doctor as soon as possible, and she was pleased when the secretary told her of a cancellation for the following day. The secretary told me of her impression that Mrs B showed a degree of anxiety in total disproportion to the account of Bridget's behaviour.

Mrs B came for the appointment with Bridget and Mr B. Bridget seemed an unremarkable twelve-year-old, reasonably well dressed, of average height and pleasant appearance. Mrs B looked extremely tense and Mr B seemed bemused, as if not quite sure where this venture would lead. They had both grown up in the neighbourhood where they now lived and their families of origin had known each other for decades. Mr B worked in building construction and Mrs B had occasional cleaning jobs. They had two younger children and they were keen to convey how normal and ordinary the family had been until the present crisis over Bridget had disrupted the image of easy-going normality.

We spent some time together and I thought that none of them was prepared to go beyond the details of Bridget's stealing and truanting. I might have continued the meeting in the same way, but, having in mind the secretary's impression, I suggested that I should speak to Bridget on her own—they all agreed to this.

Bridget proved quite difficult to engage in a conversation. I asked about school, neighbourhood, family life, and to all questions she answered with monosyllables. She liked her brother, aged nine, and she also had a four-year-old sister; they would occasionally get her into trouble, but they were essentially nice siblings. Her life at primary school had always been very happy. She had only joined secondary school a few months ago and, though she did not have a best friend, she had many friends there, including many children who had attended the same primary school as she had. She had never had problems with her teachers and, as far as she knew, they thought of her as a good student, even if she was not particularly successful academically.

Bridget was more reticent about her parents. She was fond of them and she mentioned that "many people say I'm my father's pet". She believed they treated all children fairly and she had no complaints about their attitudes to her friends or to herself. Grandparents lived nearby and she spoke of uncles, aunts, and cousins. Why had she stolen the money from her mother's purse? She could not offer any explanation. The school had organised an outing and Bridget had gone with her peers to the zoological gardens, but she simply did not know why she had taken the money. As for the truanting, again the same: "I don't know" was all that I could get for an answer. After a while, I asked Bridget to make a drawing, while I returned to the other room to speak to her parents.

Mr and Mrs B gave me more details of their individual histories and, gradually, the discussion became rather strained and somehow stilted. I voiced my view that both Bridget and Mr B seemed to feel quite self-contained, if not comfortable, while Mrs B was visibly more anxious than both of them. Trying to choose my words and watching

my tone of voice, I asked Mrs B if it was possible that there was something else in her life that made her so anxious, since I wondered
whether Bridget's behaviour might not result from her being worried
about her mother's emotional state.

Mr B visibly tensed up and turned to his wife. Mrs B burst out
crying, quite different tears now. Struggling with her sobs, she told me
that both younger children had been ill for several years, requiring
repeated surgical interventions. On top of these painful problems, Mrs
B had just discovered that she had a tumour in her breast and, if this
was not enough, after tests and consultations, doctors had recommended she should have a hysterectomy. These investigations were

Figure 1. Bridget's first drawing.

Figure 2.   Bridget's second drawing.

still going on, and Mrs B felt quite terrified that she might not have that much life ahead of her. It was difficult to know what to say at this point. Mr B held his wife's hand, trying to comfort her.

After some minutes, when Mrs B seemed more in control of herself, I suggested bringing Bridget into the room. She had made a drawing (see Figure 1) showing a landscape with some few birds and bare trees, except for one with a few scattered fruit; a blue sky with the sun and clouds was firmly separated from the landscape, and, at the bottom of the page, Bridget had drawn a lake where a couple of ducks swam in a circle of water, again sharply cut off from the rest of the lake. She could not explain what story might be depicted in the drawing. Another picture (Figure 2) showed the various members of the family and she had written their names over their heads (in the case of her brothers, the names have been removed for reasons of confidentiality).

I showed the drawings to Mr and Mrs B and invited their comments: they praised Bridget for the quality of the drawings, but could not advance any views on the subjects depicted. I again asked Bridget for comments, but she just shrugged her shoulders. I said that I thought the colourful picture seemed to suggest that one can only see what is apparent; that is, that Bridget might be indicating that whatever one thought of the ducks, there was no way of knowing what was going on beneath the surface of the lake. Again taking care with my tone of voice, I said that the way she had depicted herself in the family drawing appeared to suggest she did not quite feel a member

Figure 3. Bridget's drawings superimposed.

of the family. Bridget began to cry. I put the two drawings on top of each other (Figure 3) and I showed Bridget how the tree with fruit seemed to duplicate the spots she had drawn on her face, but in some way creating the impression of tears. And her mother was completely superimposed with the other front-line tree, but because this tree was so bare I was left with the impression that she might be wondering if anything was happening to her mother. Her reply took her parents by surprise: now crying quite painfully, Bridget said that she knew her mother was ill, since her aunt had told her of this, but she had no real idea of what the illness was.

Both Bridget and Mrs B were now turning to the box of tissues, whilst Mr B looked very pained, but clearly relieved to see that, at long last, mother and daughter had moved closer to each other.

We arranged to meet again. When I saw the family two weeks later, I was told that Bridget was "much better", attending school regularly, and much more supportive of her mother. I saw them a third time and the improvement had been maintained. Apparently, Mrs B's doctors had decided to postpone surgery and she felt more relaxed about her condition.

Comment

Considering the drawings individually, the message that Bridget felt excluded from the family is fairly clearly expressed in the second drawing. As for the first picture, the idea that only what is on the surface of the water is totally visible might be inferred from what Bridget's parents had told me about her mother's health problems. But the crucial message that Bridget was worried about her mother's health only became recognisable when the two pictures were superimposed: the happy, smiling image of her mother was now sited inside a bare, empty tree.

It might be argued that, having been told by the parents of Mrs B's illnesses and informed of their belief that Bridget did not know what was happening, one might infer that Bridget's behaviour was a reaction, an external manifestation of her concerns and anxieties. However, when these anxieties are identified and articulated on the basis of Bridget's drawings, this is more meaningful and carries a special kind of loving communication.

Evelyn

Mrs E consulted a child psychoanalyst because of her anxiety that Evelyn might be showing signs of some serious problem. Evelyn was "sleepwalking", but Mrs E thought this did not fit her image of what sleepwalking involved, hence her seeking advice. The analyst recommended analytic treatment and, because of the family's address, she suggested they should approach me, since the Clinic where I worked was sited near the Es' home.

When Mr and Mrs E came with Evelyn to the Clinic, we were told that Evelyn had began to "sleepwalk" some three months earlier. She first presented this symptom for about two weeks at the end of a school term, but then it disappeared during the following holidays. Over the month before coming to the Clinic, Evelyn had again started to walk in a sleeping state. She would walk around the house with her arms stretched out, getting hold of whatever was on her way. She would grip something and could not be prised loose. These episodes also occurred when the family went out for rides in their car. Evelyn would suddenly fall asleep and remain in this state for a long while, without the parents managing to wake her up. Sometimes, it also happened that Evelyn would fall into a deep sleep when sitting with her parents in the sitting room. Strikingly, however, when she went to sleep at night on her own bed, there had never been any similar difficulties.

Evelyn was a tall, well-built, intelligent, and articulate girl. She was now nine years old and, like other children from that upper middle-class background, had taken entrance exams for some of the local private schools. There were good indications that she would be offered a place at the school with the highest academic standards, but Evelyn was anxious lest she was not able to cope with their expectations. Evelyn told us about her life at home and at school, but, after some time, I thought that she would not voice any thoughts or feelings that she believed might hurt or antagonise her parents. I decided to take Evelyn to my own room and left her parents with the Clinic's psychiatric social worker.

Mr and Mrs E told my colleague of their family history and described Evelyn's early development. They were in their mid-thirties. Mr E had a senior position in the business world and Mrs E devoted herself to bringing up her children. Evelyn had one brother, five years old, and a sister aged three, who were described as normal and well functioning. Evelyn had shown considerable jealousy when the next sibling was born, but the youngest one was treated "as her own live doll". The parents felt that Evelyn had never given cause for anxiety, having reached her developmental milestones very normally. When we considered each parent's history, there did not seem to be anything relevant to Evelyn's present problems.

When alone with me in my room, Evelyn seemed to relax and quickly make herself at home, but I could not find any pointers to areas that might represent conflict. I offered her paper and some pens and suggested she might want to make a drawing. She drew a colourful picture (Figure 4) beginning with a rather angular and unusual looking swan and gradually developing into a scene which she described as taking place on a piece of land the family own on the continent. She drew the sun and then the bank by the river and a hut on the right of the picture, explaining that this was "like the one we have". She then drew her father fishing, a railway going through the back of the plot and also a bridge with a gate. The family car was the last element to complete this supposedly idyllic scene. Evelyn told me of the many happy days she has lived with her family in that country retreat, with no sign of conflict or unhappiness. I came to recognise that we had gone as far as we could with that picture. I decided to suggest a second picture.

Evelyn looked at the blank page, thought for a bit, and, with a happy chuckle, informed me that she would make a drawing where she would employ all the letters of the alphabet. She began with a very large "A" (Figure 5) and as soon as she depicted the "b" that made it into a wigwam, a tone of excitement crept into her voice, as she announced each following letter; the "c" turned out to be also a

Figure 4. Evelyn's first drawing.

Figure 5.   Evelyn's second drawing.

"d" when seen together with the vertical arm of the "b", and I took this as a warning that elements could change in their meaning, depending on how they were considered. Unfortunately, I would not be able to identify each letter that followed, but it must be significant that the "I" was depicted as the spears used by the Indians (shown inside the "G", near the tree on the left of the picture). A cowboy has been tied to the tree and, on the opposite side of the picture, three male Indians are shown around the cauldron on the fire.

Evelyn explained that these Indians had wives. Each of the three wives had three children and they were all inside the wigwam. As she moved to the end of the alphabet, there was mounting excitement. The Indians were seen as the "baddies" and their chief, mounted on a horse, merited more detailed comments on how aggressive and vindictive he was. We looked together at the drawings and discussed the marked contrast of their contents. The violence and impending killing in the picture with the Indians did not have any obvious connection with the bucolic peacefulness of the first drawing.

I now put the two drawings on top of each other, explaining to Evelyn that this would represent a pretence that the two were like one picture. I emphasised that it was not a question of making things match, but of ensuring that the corners of each page were precisely on top of each other. I then lifted the joint pages and held them against the light coming from the nearby window (Figure 6). Evelyn commented that the swan was now inside the wigwam. I called her attention to the overlap between the Indian chief and her father: she was very surprised and her face showed embarrassment. She did not know what to make of this. I asked her if it was possible that she was keen to keep her father as somebody very peaceful and kind, not really liking to think of him in any negative way, as the Indian chief was depicted. She lowered her head and, very quietly, confirmed that this was true. After a pause, Evelyn told me of arguments that occasionally occur between her parents and how frightened she becomes by them. She felt that invariably one of them would be on her side, defending her from the other parent. I suggested that on those occasions, she might well feel that her father could become violent, like the Indian chief. She now smiled, saying this was quite true and proceeded to emphasise the way in which his tone and volume of voice will change, making his words sound very threatening.

We rejoined the parents and the social worker, and I explained that I thought Evelyn's sleep-walking was probably due to emotional

Figure 6. Evelyn's drawings superimposed.

factors, but, considering the intensity of their worries and the unusual presentation of the symptom, I recommended we should request a paediatric assessment. Mr and Mrs E were very pleased with this idea and eventually we had a report that nothing physical had been found that might be causing the sleeping disturbances presented by Evelyn.

I saw Evelyn a few weeks later. We discussed her progress and she asked to make a drawing (not shown here). This showed how people can deal with dangerous situations in different ways and Evelyn recognised her view that one of the most effective ways to detach oneself from danger is to shut one's eyes, and she smiled, recognising the link with her sleeping episodes. She was able to articulate how frightened her father can make her feel.

When I saw the parents on their own two weeks later, they reported that there had not been any further episodes of sleep-walking. In fact, they talked as if they had virtually forgotten about those incidents. They could not establish with any precision when they had last occurred. After some thought, Mrs E burst out laughing and said that perhaps the last one had taken place when they had visited the paediatrician. She laughed heartily when admitting that she did not want to attach much importance to the interviews with me. The family atmosphere had obviously improved dramatically. The couple went on to tell me that Evelyn had now developed a new symptom: it was impossible to rouse her in the mornings and she was practically asleep until she was sitting at table, having her breakfast. But before I could comment on this, Mrs E told me that, in fact, her husband had exactly the same difficulties in the mornings.

I saw Evelyn a few more times over the ensuing months. There were no episodes of sleep-walking and the troubles in the morning had also disappeared. Evelyn obtained a place in the school with the higher academic standards and she settled down well in her new class.

Comment

Focusing on each drawing separately, one would certainly conclude that Evelyn was trying hard to keep under control an ambivalent view of the world in which she lived. It was only when the two pictures were superimposed that Evelyn could recognise and admit to the anxieties related to her perception of her father as someone who could lose his temper and behave in a frightening manner. Presumably, she found that my reaction enabled her to articulate feelings and fantasies that she had learnt to keep under tight control. Perhaps these were not completely unconscious sentiments, but subsequent developments clearly demonstrated that her "sleep-walking" was the only way in which she had managed to make herself and the world know that she was struggling with feelings that she could not cope with. Finding a way of expressing her anxieties and perhaps recognising herself the extent of her fears helped her to abandon the "sleep-walking" symptom/language through which they were making their presence known.

Betty

The mother of this ten-year-old girl asked for help because she could not cope with Betty's constant defiance and rebellion. An older son and two younger daughters were described as pleasant and friendly, though Betty quite often provoked the sisters into arguments and fights. Apparently, Betty presented no problems at school and had a normal, active social life with neighbours and friends.

We were told that Mrs B had divorced her husband shortly after the birth of the youngest child. They continued to have a friendly relationship and Mrs B spoke warmly of her ex-husband's new wife. But out of her four children, it was Betty who kept harking back to the days when she lived with her father. Mrs B described a recent occasion when she got so angry with Betty that she asked her ex-husband to have the girl staying with him for a few days. Apparently, Betty loved this and her behaviour at home improved—for a few days . . .

When I met Betty, I found it quite difficult to establish a dialogue with her. It emerged that her mother had told her that the reason for coming to see me was so that she could discuss with me which secondary school she should go to. But Betty felt quite happy with her choice of school and, in fact, she was convinced that she would have no trouble in being accepted there. Gradually, we managed to widen the focus of the conversation and Betty was able to tell me that she and her siblings were quite happy with their parents' separation, since they had remained good friends, even though when they lived under the same roof they just had endless fights.

I asked Betty if she would perhaps make a drawing. As in similar consultations, I had a drawing pad and some pens and pencils on the desk. Betty hesitated for some moments and then drew two faces (Figure 7). I asked why the large face had empty eyes, but she just shrugged her shoulders, adding, "I don't know . . ." Considering the expressions on the faces, I asked how she saw them and she wrote down "young, happy", and scribbled over the beginning of a third word that she could not tell what it was meant to be. She added "old, happy" next to the smaller face. Again, we had the same difficulty in getting a conversation going and I suggested she might make another drawing. She turned the pages of the pad and eventually drew the girl (Figure 8) whom she described as "girl, gay", but, again, no further comments.

I decided to try to see what happened if the two pages were superimposed (Figure 9), and I found that the girl's head fitted in with the young man's eye. I explained my "manoeuvre" as a way of pretending that the two drawings were, actually, one. I asked Betty what she thought of the resulting image. She thought about it and as I was looking for the words to describe the position of the girl's head inside the man's eye, Betty said, "She is the apple of his eye". After a pause, I asked if that was how she believed her father saw her. "Yes, I do," she replied.

Figure 7.   Betty's first drawing.

Figure 8.   Betty's second drawing.

Figure 9.   Betty's drawings superimposed.

I saw Betty for another interview and this time she spoke a bit more freely about her feelings towards her parents. She was pleased that they had remained friends and she regretted that when they lived together they had so many clashes. She told me a bit about her feelings towards her siblings, but the fundamental point was her contention that she did not need any help. She was certain that she would obtain a place in the school she wanted and she felt quite content in her circle of friends and colleagues. For her part, Mrs B arranged to have private appointments with a psychotherapist and only got in touch with us some months later to report that Betty seemed to be a happier girl and that the two of them seldom had the clashes that had given rise to the approach to the Clinic.

Comment

Looking at Betty's drawings, it is possible to argue that the superimposition of the man's eye and the girl's head was no more than a coincidence, but it still enabled Betty to endorse the resulting obvious interpretation of this superimposition. Betty's wish to be her father's favourite child was probably not unconscious, but she certainly had not allowed this hope to become an overt communication. Was this helpful to her? Perhaps this is a matter of opinion, but developments following the interview certainly pointed in that direction. It is conceivable that having another older person know of her "secret" feelings helped Betty not to feel guilty about harbouring them.

Here we have a clear example of how drawings can be used as a language through which to split and express feelings that are kept secret—not that there is necessarily a definite conscious wish to convey these feelings, but apparently there is an unconscious recognition of finding a setting, a context, in which these "forbidden" feelings can be expressed.

Daniel

I was asked to see Daniel when he was seven and a half years old. He had been encopretic since the age of three, and his mother told me that he had not responded to many prescriptions and techniques that different professionals had recommended over the years. Daniel had a three and a half-year-old brother. Daniel had attended a local nursery and now was at a small private primary school, and all his teachers had always spoken of him in glowing terms: he made good academic progress and his relationship to teachers and peers was excellent. Mrs D had tried to establish some correlation between the messing and other factors in Daniel's life, but she was not convinced there was any such link. Chronologically, Daniel's soiling had started around the time that his parents' marriage broke down, but Mrs D argued against this being more than a coincidence. The soiling only occurred at home, usually when Daniel returned from school, and Mrs D just about managed to consider there might be a link between the symptom and her presence, but she still insisted that the soiling might happen if Daniel was away from her for some length of time, something that had never taken place.

Mrs D came to the interview with Daniel and his younger brother. The little boy managed to occupy himself with a few toys and remained virtually silent throughout the meeting, quite ignored by Daniel and their mother. Daniel quickly moved to a table where he found a dolls' house, toys, paper, and some felt-tip pens. He answered questions I put to him easily and in a friendly tone of voice, but without showing much interest in establishing a conversation. Mrs D, however ... well, she was virtually unstoppable! I assumed that Daniel must have known that his mother tended to hold the floor and, accordingly, stepped back.

Daniel explored various toys, but he soon concentrated on making some drawings. I noticed his preference for dark colours and noted that he seemed to keep up a running commentary about what he was drawing, but instead of asking him to speak louder, I decided to learn from Mrs D something about the family's history.

Mrs D was a very attractive woman. She came from continental Europe and was passionate and intense in her speech, using her face and body to emphasise the nuances and implications of each story she told me. She did reply to any questions I put to her, but I often felt that she fitted my questions into some pre-established rota; at other times, it seemed as if she was moving from subject to subject, following some associative link that she might be unable to identify, if challenged about it. Although we were meeting early in the morning, Mrs D was elaborately made-up. She clearly had her own style of speaking and relating. The children's appearance suggested that she had taught them how to look after their clothes and how to behave in the presence of a stranger. And, yet, here I was being told of Daniel's encopresis and also that his brother still wet his bed every night. Considering that all through her account Mrs D not once addressed her children, I ended up wondering whether, however punctilious about their social presentation, Mrs D did not have much awareness of their emotional needs and sensitivities.

Mrs D was an only child. Her father had left the family when she was still very young and she had spent most of her childhood in a kind of boarding school. She told me with considerable enthusiasm about her work experience, visiting exciting places and meeting interesting people, one of whom had been Daniel's father.

Daniel's father was described as a gentle and quiet Englishman. They had married and lived together in Mrs D's country of origin, where they were very happy. Somehow, they decided to live in England, but, soon after arriving here, conflicts started. Eventually, the marriage broke down when Daniel was three years old, but Mrs D had no intention of returning to her home country. Daniel saw his father on alternate weekends and he told me that he enjoyed the time they spent together.

Mrs D remarried one year later and her second son was born some months afterwards. According to Mrs D, her second husband had not managed to win Daniel over and, in fact, they had a very fraught relationship. I wondered what role the encopresis played in this picture, and Mrs D told me that Daniel's father thought it was "up to her" to deal with all the consequences of this problem.

When I mentioned the little boy's enuresis, Mrs D dismissed it out of hand. She told me that, yes, there were times when she was annoyed and impatient at having to deal with it, but the little boy was only three and a half years old and she did not want to make too much of a fuss about a symptom that she was convinced would disappear sooner or later. I did not feel able to raise the question of what the little boy himself might feel about this symptom.

By now, Daniel began to show signs of restlessness. He had made several drawings and he was obviously keen to tell me about them. I apologised to Mrs D and turned my attention to Daniel. His brother continued to play by himself and Mrs D now concentrated on following Daniel's account and my questions and comments about what he told me. It was quite fascinating to discover that, as soon as I made myself available to him, Daniel moved on to a crescendo of feelings and speed in his account. It was not that he lost control, since he was able to stop and listen to me when I indicated I had something to say. He was checking to make sure that I understood what he was telling me. Nevertheless, it was very striking how the quiet and thoughtful boy could gradually shift into a mode of delivery that entirely duplicated that of his mother's.

Daniel drew material (Figure 10) from a television feature that dominated children's lives at the time of our meeting. He told me the names of the various spaceships and explained what characterised each of them: a huge Millennium Falcon belonged to the goodies and this was under attack from a Star Dish Destroyer and a Death Star. An X-wing fighter had come to help the Millennium Falcon, but the Death Star had just fired a laser gun on the Falcon—this missed the craft, "passed underneath it". Daniel explained that soon a further laser shot was to be fired on the X-wing and on other crafts.

The second picture he had made (Figure 11) showed ET, the friendly extra-terrestrial, standing on Earth, looking utterly miserable

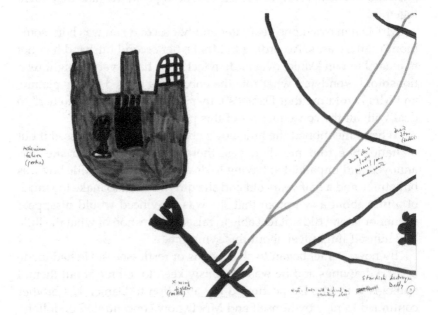

Figure 10.   Daniel's first drawing.

Figure 11.   Daniel's second drawing.

and hopeless. The door of his spaceship is about to close and leave him behind. A very heavy and menacing sky has its blackness barely mellowed by a yellow moon. Daniel made a third drawing (Figure 12) showing Superman, exuding self-confidence, standing beside a sky-scraper that is, clearly, no challenge to him. I looked attentively at each drawing and Daniel was happy to explain the difference between the hopeless, if lovable, ET and the all-powerful Superman.

I decided to check what would happen if we superimposed the two first drawings. I put the two sheets of paper, carefully matching their corners, on top of each other and examined them against the light coming in from the window. Daniel looked at the superimposed images and thought the result was quite amusing (Figure 13): ET was now the victim of the laser beam shots coming from the baddies. Daniel burst out laughing and, after the briefest of pauses, launched into the account of a recent dream, where he was being chased by a witch. There seemed to be no end to the dream! Daniel was going through tunnels, with the witch in his pursuit. No sooner did he manage to leave one tunnel, he found himself inside another one, and the witch was again behind him "holding a broom with which she

Figure 12.   Daniel's third drawing.

tried to hit me and cast a spell to turn me into an ant". At this point, I called his attention to the shape of the X-wing fighter: it looks like a broom and Daniel fleetingly nodded his head to indicate his apparent agreement, but he was really engrossed in the account of the dream. He explained that one of the tunnels was full of ants and there was also a river with a high tree by the water, from which he jumped to the other bank, and endless more details that emphasised how dangerous this chase was.

Mrs D had been following this story with mixed feelings. On the one hand, she seemed fascinated by the steps Daniel was follow-ing from the drawings to the account of the dream, but, at the same time, there was some irritation or embarrassment, which led her to attempt to interrupt and stop Daniel's endless story. But, eventually, Daniel did stop. He had arrived at the end of the dream and he now looked at me for some feedback. I considered the superimposed drawings and thought that the laser shot that had missed the Millen-

Figure 13.   Daniel's first and second drawings superimposed.

nium Falcon had, in fact, struck not only ET on the other page, but also the broom-like, helpful X-wing fighter, which I now was inclined to see as a representation of his mother. Only later did I remember Mrs D's interruptions and I wondered whether this might be some kind of re-enactment of the dream; that is, the witch trying to stop Daniel.

But I did not voice any of these thoughts based on the drawings. I opted, instead, to focus on his dream. I told Daniel that I thought the tunnels, the river, and all the scary components of his attempt to run away from a threatening witch represented his idea of what went on inside his tummy. Daniel beamed and looked at his mother, as if hoping for an acknowledgement. But Mrs D was too surprised at my comment and she could not quite hide her disbelief at the absurdity of what I had said. I called her attention to Daniel's obvious, explicit agreement with my interpretation and Mrs D decided not to question what I was saying.

I explained to Mrs D (and Daniel!) that the body functions need external help before they can achieve a regular, independent rhythm. Daniel's problems did result from his imaginings about what went on inside his tummy, but he needed help from her in order to normalise his bowel functions. I urged her to put him on the toilet morning and evening, always at the same times, to help him overcome his fears and achieve his own rhythm of defecating. I also explained about the advisability of keeping a diary, giving him points for success and taking points off for failure, all aiming at a reward they would agree on. Mrs D smiled and said she would "give it a try".

We made a follow-up appointment for three weeks later, but Mrs D telephoned the Clinic the previous day to say that this was quite unnecessary. From the same day of the appointment, Daniel had not messed himself again. She had already given him the reward they had agreed he would receive after two clean weeks and he was now convinced he would get a new present after another clean week.

Much to my gratified surprise, Mrs D insisted the secretary should tell me that she was sure the messing had disappeared "because of what (I) had told him". She said she could not believe this was possible, but she had to recognise the facts.

Several weeks later, the Health Visitor confirmed that the initial progress had been maintained.

Comment

I do believe that it was Daniel seeing the superimposition of his drawings that made him recognise and remember the contents of his dreams. The imagery his unconscious had resorted to in the dreams was very different to that employed in the drawings, but in both we have the baddies persecuting the goodies—Daniel's unconscious fantasy of being the victim of his mother's demands and injunctions: an interpretation that might explain the striking timing and placing of Daniel's encopresis. However, we must also assume that Mrs D did change her approach to Daniel and managed to make him see that instead of being only the "persecuting witch", she could become the helpful mother, enabling him to achieve bowel control. Together with Daniel's relief at discovering and understanding what his dreams indicated, this would explain how he succeeded in achieving the normality of his body function.

Felix

Felix had been involved in serious problems at school because of his aggressive behaviour. Teachers had tried various stratagems to help him to control his temper, but they had no success. To make matters worse, when the school addressed Mrs F and attempted to enlist her help, she turned against the teachers, accusing them of discriminating against Felix and blaming them for his behaviour. The school and the educational psychologist called for a series of meetings between teachers and Mrs F, but these had also been totally unsuccessful in achieving any resolution of the conflicts. Referral to the child psychiatrist was the next suggestion made by the school, and Mrs F, reluctantly, accepted this.

Predictably, ours was a "gauche" meeting. Whatever I might say, I was still seen as an agent of the school. I was seeing Felix at a Child Guidance Clinic and this was, in fact, part of the educational facilities for the community. In practice, I had to be extra careful with my questions, as both Felix and his mother had no intention of revealing anything that they considered to be unrelated to behaviour at school. My usual procedure of trying to obtain a family history and to probe the child and parents on issues that might help me to compose a picture of their interactions here had to be abandoned in favour of direct, clear questions focusing on Felix's relationship with his peers.

Felix was thirteen. He had gone through his primary school years without difficulties and, apparently, only after starting secondary education at eleven did he begin to clash with teachers and peers. His academic progress was only moderate, but this seemed to be seen as commensurate with his abilities. It was Felix's behaviour and general attitudes that brought him to the attention of his teachers. However, these problems escalated after Felix had an accident at school, falling on an apparatus when playing a game with other boys. His face was badly cut and this required surgical attention. Sadly, he was left with a scar on his cheek and before long his peers discovered that they could upset Felix by calling him "Scar face", "Frankenstein", or other similar names.

Mrs F told me that she had a job in the neighbourhood and this enabled her to bring up her children without major difficulties. Her marriage had broken down some years earlier, but Mrs F did not wish to give me any further information about this. She saw Felix as a good, average, normal boy and she emphasised that her whole family were fond of him, all of which was meant to underline her view that Felix's problems were entirely related to his school life. She could acknowledge that puberty was a difficult time for a youngster, and Felix was just starting puberty. He sat quietly near his mother and I had the impression that he would never say anything that he assumed might upset her.

I mentioned to Felix that he could make a drawing. He hesitated and asked me to give him a theme. I suggested he made a picture of himself (Figure 14). This showed very prominently the scar that so bothered him. There would, obviously, be no point in my commenting that it did not strike me as so noticeable as the picture indicated it felt to him. I was feeling quite at a loss as to how to proceed. I was sure that Felix's sense of outrage at being called names could not be entirely due to the scar on his face. His tone of voice contained an element of insecurity and vulnerability, which might be due to the

Figure 14. Felix's first drawing.

circumstances in which we were meeting, but the account that Felix and his mother gave of his life in the family and in the community seemed to suggest some sense of self-confidence that should have helped him not to become such an easy prey to the teasing and taunting of his school peers. That he should prove to be such an easy victim made me wonder whether there were other wounds that were being touched by his schoolmates.

It happened that I had noticed right from our first moments together that Mrs F also had a scar under her eye. I did not feel able to ask her what this was due to, probably because of the many barriers Mrs F had put forward, resisting any kind of personal probing. Writing this account, I feel I should be able to offer an explanation for what followed next, but this would always be a *post facto* inference, rather than a true account of what went on in my conscious mind. I asked Felix whether he would be able to make a drawing of his mother. He smiled, embarrassed, and Mrs F looked amused and perhaps even curious, if not flattered at such a suggestion.

Felix drew his mother without any difficulty (Figure 15). She was delighted at the beautiful smile he had put on her face and Felix clearly appreciated her pleasure. I looked at the drawing,

Figure 15.   Felix's second drawing.

complimented him on the ease with which he had done it, and voiced some pleasant adjectives about the picture, but then, after a pause, I put the two drawings together, one on top of the other and showed this to Felix (Figure 16). He was surprised, and stressed that he had not meant them to be so similarly located on the page. I said to Felix that I was struck by the fact that the superimposition of the drawings showed a scar under his mother's eyes that he had not drawn in the picture meant to depict her. To my total amazement, he burst out crying.

Figure 16.   Felix's drawings superimposed.

Mrs F was embarrassed by this unexpected development, but she managed a smile and told me that this was not a scar, but an area of discoloration of her skin. I guess Felix spoke before thinking, but he said he had always thought this was a scar resulting from multiple beatings she had suffered from a man-friend who had lived with them when he was six years old. Mrs F was profoundly disturbed by this statement. She said that she had never known that Felix had any memories of those events or that he had been so intensely affected by them.

I had opened a real Pandora's box. I did voice my view that Felix needed psychotherapeutic help to make sense of his past and present experiences, but I found that Mrs F would never agree to further interviews with me or anyone else. Rightly or wrongly, I was certain that as soon as Felix and his mother left my room the lid would be closed on the box Felix had momentarily opened.

Mrs F accepted another appointment, but did not attend. Follow-up information from the school was that Felix continued to be seen as a boy in need of help.

Comment

It is impossible to know how this interview would have evolved if Felix had not made his two drawings and I had not made the comments I made when seeing the superimposition of the two pictures. I am sure that the emotional impact my question had on Felix was due to his recognising that, even if he had overtly respected his mother's feelings by not drawing the abnormality of the skin under her eyes, his unconscious had put forward a pointer to his awareness of that abnormality and what it meant to him. Felix had expressed in drawings the presence of sentiments and memories that he would never put into spoken words. Only by splitting into two separate pictures his feelings about his own and his mother's scars was he able to express the presence and the nature of his traumatic memories.

Barbara

The general practitioner referred this "intelligent ten-year-old" because "for the last four months, since her baby brother was born,"

Barbara had "become increasingly anxious; she hates being separated from her parents and fears being left." The GP thought this was probably linked to "sibling jealousy". The parents were alarmed by the intensity of the girl's fears, but they also felt some irritation at the way in which Barbara's complaints were interfering with family life.

Mrs B was obviously foreign; an attractive round face, sensuous lips and eyes, very black hair, and an easy smile, but neither her appearance nor her accent would enable one to guess where she came from. She was holding a lovely eight-month-old baby, who smiled and then slept peacefully through our meeting. Barbara looked like a miniature version of her mother, but her attractive face and her friendly smile did not hide completely her tension and a degree of fear about what this interview might signify. Mrs B explained that Barbara had not wanted to come, but she agreed to do so "only this once".

Mrs B told me of their country of origin—one of the world's trouble spots. Mrs B told me that Barbara had become terribly clinging, panicking when the mother moved away or was delayed when picking her up from school. Mrs B thought this might be due to the closeness that had developed between them when Mr B was abroad for a whole year. They had visited Mr B abroad and that was when Mrs B became pregnant. As her pregnancy progressed, Barbara had become a faithful companion, watching over her, helping in any manner she could, and proving to be an almost indispensable presence. When Mr B returned home, Barbara was happy, but at the same time "she felt displaced", said Mrs B.

Mrs B gave me innumerable examples of Barbara's clinging: she followed her mother to the bathroom, she was afraid of going to sleep and demanded one of her parents should stay with her until she fell asleep, protested if Mrs B stayed too long with the baby in her arms, resented her father being too affectionate with the baby, she came to the parents' bedroom in the night, watched at the window when her father was due to arrive back home, became tearful if either parent went out for shopping or for other reasons—but the idea that all this had followed the birth of the baby seemed to be a conclusion they had arrived at only in hindsight.

These examples were given throughout the interview, coming from either Mrs B or Barbara herself. Some stories were recounted with expressions of amusement and others with bafflement, reflecting the varying emotions that phobic behaviour tends to arouse in those who live with the identified patient. We consider a clinging child and we then find an adult who oscillates between over-protection and behaviour that the child experiences as overt or covert rejection.

One of the situations that had most puzzled Barbara's parents had occurred outside home and had been triggered by an apparently minor stimulus: in preparation for school exams, Barbara had to attend lessons at her tutor's place. Her parents used to drop her there, go off to do some shopping, and then pick her up again. After the baby's birth, it was Mr B who drove Barbara. Presumably, she had assumed that he stayed in the car, waiting for the end of the lesson, because one day when he said he would go and have a drink, though he would be back in the car by the time the lesson was finished, Barbara just went to pieces. She cried and pleaded with her father to stay there and as her distress mounted, she asked him to come in and stay at the teacher's flat for the lesson. After this episode, the parents had considered whether they should have the teacher come to their house for the lessons.

It was not difficult to engage Barbara in conversation. She had initially smiled, rather embarrassed, and her mother had taken the initiative to tell me some of the above stories, but when I tried to get Barbara herself to speak, she warmed up and tried to answer my questions. She told me about school, teachers and friends—no problems anywhere, she was a good student and a popular girl. She could speak her parents' mother tongue, in spite of having been born in this country. She told me about relations who lived around London and she was up to date with the life of those others who lived in various parts of the world. She told me that her mother had obtained a university degree and worked as a teacher until the baby's birth. When I asked what work her father did, Barbara said she did not know what it was. She was hesitating, perhaps embarrassed, and I could not guess why this was so. Barbara turned to her mother and I asked Mrs B not to "help" her at this point. Both of them were puzzled by my request and I explained that I had no doubt that Mrs B would be able to give me the factual, correct answer to my question, but, at that point, I would prefer to learn of what Barbara made of the world she lived in. Mrs B accepted this and Barbara smiled, hesitated a bit, and decided to do as I had requested. "Well . . . I think . . . he works for Mr X" (she gave me a name), she said, looking at her mother for confirmation. Mrs B said this was not correct, but I asked her again to leave for a bit later the correction she obviously wanted to make. I knew that Mr X was an eminent figure in the parents' country of origin and I thought to myself that their nationality and Mr B's job might be relevant to understand Barbara's anxieties.

Barbara now told me, in her own words, of her fears. She could only say that she was afraid that her mother might leave her behind and she told me of what had happened the previous day. Every Wednesday she has music lessons at school, and she knew that her mother would be at the gate waiting for her when she came out at 5 p.m. Mrs B always tells her that she arrives there some fifteen minutes before five, and the previous day it happened that the class finished earlier. Barbara waited outside and she expected her mother to arrive at 4.45 p.m. Once this time came, she began to experience mounting anxiety and, even if she knew that her mother would not let her down, she was in quite a panic by the time Mrs B got to the school. She explained that she usually felt no similar fears over her father's presence or absence. Barbara agreed with her mother that her symptoms appeared to date from the birth of the baby.

I had formed, by now, some idea of the content of Barbara's anxieties, but I thought I would like to find stronger evidence to substantiate my theory. I felt that further questions to Barbara would not produce the evidence I was after and I asked her to make some drawing for me. She smiled, rather surprised at the request, and I explained that I would like to ask Mrs B for information about the family history and that she "might prefer" to draw while we talked. Indeed, not the whole truth, but all children appear to accept this as a valid explanation. Barbara moved to a little desk in the room, arranging paper and pens and making herself comfortable.

Mrs B told me that her husband came from an illustrious family and, from very early in his life, he had decided to follow in the footsteps of his male predecessors. He was educated in what his family considered one of the world's centres of academic excellence. For her part, Mrs B came from a middle-class family; her father brought up his children to be active, contributing members of society, but he was more preoccupied with a moral and humanistic angle than with political or military involvement. Mrs B had married her husband twelve years earlier, when he had returned home to visit his family. When Mr B was appointed to an important job abroad, the couple moved there and Mrs B took advantage of this to further her education and obtain a university degree. After some time, her husband moved from the public to the private sector. He was seen as an expert in organisation and management and in a short time he had signed contracts with several people, including Mr X.

Mrs B was convinced that Barbara's anxieties were totally centred on the changes that the baby's birth had brought to the family's life. Her description of her own and her husband's life reflected her view of a lifestyle that she considered typical of many other modern big-city couples where the husbands were top executives. He had an irregular schedule of working hours, he travelled a lot, there were continuous telephone and fax messages (no mobiles or computers in the days when I saw them . . .) demanding answers or attendances at meetings, meal times were never regular or uneventful, parties had to be cancelled—but she thought this was not abnormal.

However, I was aware that at the time of this interview there were probably a dozen countries with one or more Mr Xs requiring the assistance of one or more Mr Bs! Latin America, the Middle East, the Far East, many parts of Africa, and some European countries as well. At this point of the interview, I had, however, no evidence to suggest that any of these thoughts were relevant to explain Barbara's anxieties, but I was still reasonably convinced that she was afraid of losing sight of her parents in case they suffered any damage in the hands of some enemy. But how could I find the evidence for this? I could only hope that Barbara's drawing might give us some clues to clarify my suspicions. She had, in fact, made two drawings.

The first drawing (Figure 17) showed a doll standing on its feet. Barbara laughed when I asked where she had got the idea for this doll, pointing to a shelf in the room on which sat a rag doll: she had seen its reflection on a mirror near her table. "But that doll on the shelf is sitting down," I said. "Oh, I cannot draw dolls sitting down," said Barbara. She had, actually, finished this first drawing while I was talking to Mrs B, so I suggested she might make another one. She hesitated for a few seconds and then picked up a second sheet of paper, which she laid on top of the first one. When I saw the second drawing (Figure 18), I wondered whether Barbara had traced it over the first one. She denied this, explaining that she always makes her drawings in this manner, selecting individual sheets, which she carefully lays out on top of the preceding picture, but "I never trace pictures," she said.

Figure 17.   Barbara's first drawing.

Figure 18.   Barbara's second drawing.

The second drawing showed two flowers, one vertical and the other horizontal. I asked about them and she said they were daffodils, adding that she had done a project on these flowers a few days earlier at school. I asked about the layout, but Barbara shrugged her shoulders, saying there was no particular reason for her choosing to draw them in that particular way. I put the two pictures on top of each other, carefully matching all corners, and held them against the light for Barbara to see the result. Barbara and her mother looked at the perfect superimposition (Figure 19) of the doll and the standing daffodil and their faces showed surprise and puzzlement. They said nothing.

I asked Barbara what might she think of seeing a daffodil in the horizontal position she had drawn. It was Mrs B who answered that it might have withered and fallen down. I thought that the pictures had struck some chord in Mrs B and her comment sounded as if she had taken the images as her own. Barbara repeated her mother's words and added that someone might have pulled it out or else cut it off. She paused, looking rather pensively at her mother and then at me. I looked at her and I am sure my expression conveyed the underlying question of what these various possibilities implied. Barbara

Figure 19. Barbara's drawings superimposed.

said, "In any case, it would be dead." I said that she had not drawn the doll lying horizontally, but perhaps the two daffodils were depicting, as flowers, what she was afraid might happen to the doll. She nodded, indicating she knew what I meant.

I had noticed that Mrs B had voiced an eventuality where the daffodil would die a natural death, while Barbara had suggested a violent end, but I decided not to mention this. I said that Barbara was very afraid of what might happen to her mother and to her father, hence her wish to keep them both under her eyes. Barbara stared at her mother, who looked very surprised and asked Barbara for comments. Barbara nodded and confirmed she did harbour such fears. Mrs B tried to reassure her, saying that such anxieties were not necessary, but Barbara reminded her of a television programme they had seen, where a man originating from their country had been gunned down in another country. They could not remember the exact timing of the programme, but I would not be surprised if it had marked the beginning of Barbara's clinging to her parents.

There was a heavy silence in the room. Barbara and her mother looked, lovingly, at each other. Finally, Mrs B plucked up enough courage to confirm that she also shared Barbara's fears. There was no doubt that Barbara had known of this, but it had not been mentioned up to that point of our meeting. Mrs B told me that she had been trying to persuade her husband to change his work, since his eminent client was too well known in the world and this assignment exposed Mr B to risks that were intensely felt in the family. She knew, however, that this commitment meant far too much for her husband and it was unlikely that he would ever give it up.

I explained to Barbara and Mrs B that I was sure that the birth of the baby was bound to produce fears of rejection in Barbara, but both Mr and Mrs B could gradually reassure her against these. However, when it came to the question of Barbara's fears for the safety of her parents (if not for her own, as well!), sadly, neither parent could really hope to reassure her, since they knew these anxieties were well founded.

Comment

I saw Barbara and her mother a few more times. I recommended that Barbara should have individual psychotherapy, but when a vacancy materialised Barbara decided she felt better and did not wish to take this up. Mrs B confirmed that Barbara was much less anxious and coping well with ordinary daily life.

This might be one of the most striking cases of split images that I have found. As with some other cases, one might infer the nature of the child's unconscious anxieties from the data obtained in the course of the consultation, but it is still doubtful that Barbara would ever be able to articulate her fear that some disaster might occur to her father: not only was she afraid of formulating the total content of her anxieties, but she was also aware that voicing these would only lead to painful feelings in her parents. Barbara's reaction to the television programme seemed not to have been known by her mother and, presumably, Mrs B herself had also refrained from allowing Barbara to know of her own feelings about the event depicted in the film. These repressed anxieties found expression in the separate drawings that, when superimposed, showed very clearly the nature of the fears that had led to Barbara's behaviour.

Julie

This girl produced a different presentation of the split drawings, but I believe this is still a valid example of the phenomenon I am describing.

I saw Julie when she was thirteen years old. Mrs J had moved with her children to the area of the Clinic not long before I saw her with Julie. Julie had joined the local secondary school, but was finding it very difficult to adjust to the new neighbourhood. She complained of a multitude of physical symptoms, but several consultations with the local general practitioner failed to elicit any physical abnormality. Quite reluctantly, Mrs J accepted consulting the local Child Guidance Clinic.

The family had lived through very traumatic years. Apparently, Mr J not only abused alcohol, but was also violent towards his wife and children. After many years of marriage, Mrs J decided to put a stop to the marriage and left the home with the children, managing to be rehoused in a new community, quite far from where they had lived. Mrs J was trying hard to rebuild her life, but recently her children had come home to tell her that they had unexpectedly met their father in the street, and he had told them that he carried both a gun and a knife, warning them that they should report this to their mother.

Julie looked younger than her age. She did answer questions, but only in a whisper and in monosyllables. After a while, noticing that she looked quite often at the sheets of paper and pens on the desk by which she was sitting, I suggested she might make a drawing. She drew a large cat, standing in a field with plants, grass, and clouds around the sun (Figure 20). I asked her to tell me something about the cat and she said he was happy because it was such a nice, sunny day. I asked about the squiggly line on each side of the cat and she burst out laughing, but was totally unable to explain what they represented or why she was laughing. I had to accept her not knowing, but I noticed that she was still holding the pencil and I asked if she perhaps wanted to make another drawing.

Julie put the drawing aside and placed another sheet of paper in front of her. She now drew (Figure 21) a very large tree and a garden. She looked at the drawing for a time and then drew a bird on a branch of a tree. When I asked her about the house, she told me that a woman

Figure 20. Julie's first drawing.

Figure 21. Julie's second drawing.

and her two children lived in it. She said they were happy because they liked the house and the garden. There was a pause; she looked at both drawings and then added that the cat of the first drawing also lived in the same house. I asked her to enlarge on this, but she was not able to do so.

I decided to find out what would happen if we superimposed the two pictures. She had drawn the cat with the paper in a vertical position in front of her and the second drawing was made with the paper lying horizontally in front of her. I therefore put one page on top of the other, making sure that the bottom sides were perfectly matched and that the vertical page was exactly in the middle of the other one (Figure 22). To our surprise, when we looked at these drawings against the light, we found that the bird was placed exactly inside the cat's belly. Julie burst out laughing when she saw this. I asked her if she had made up any story to accompany the drawings she had made or if she had imagined anything specifically about the cat and the bird. She denied having built any story and repeated that the only thing she could say was that the cat lived in the house. So, I asked her, "What about the bird then?", and she laughed again. "Oh! It had better fly away quickly!"

Figure 22. Julie's drawings superimposed.

After a pause, I suggested that her drawings seemed to depict how happy she felt living in the new house with her mother and brother, but that she was afraid that her father (the cat) might come and spoil everything. Julie agreed that this might be the case and her mother, who had been observing closely the drawings and our conversation, said that this was precisely how she felt about their situation. Julie and Mrs J now talked about their terror that any of them might be seen in the streets by people who might report their whereabouts to Mr J. It was not surprising that both Mrs J and her children felt so insecure and tense.

Comment

I do believe that the image resulting from the superimposition of the two drawings is not a coincidence. It is very probable that Julie saw herself represented by the bird and that the cat was an image of her father as big and powerful. It is conceivable that Julie harboured secret wishes that her father might reappear and again be a presence in her life, but such an interpretation could not be raised in the context in which the interview was taking place. I chose to concentrate on the shared reality of their everyday life that brought an element of serious danger to the appearance of her father. Julie felt isolated at school and had asked her teachers to move her to the class where her friend was: the school agreed to this and the reports we had over the following months were that Julie had settled down and was much happier.

Georgia

Georgia had gone with friends to a funfair and, at some point, decided to choose a shortcut when trying to get to another part of the fair. They were passing behind one of the stalls when they suddenly found themselves confronted by a dog that jumped on them and happened to hurt Georgia's lower lip.

Georgia was intensely disturbed by this experience, but what eventually brought her to a child psychiatrist was the fact that for the ensuing two months she kept waking up at night, screaming and crying inconsolably, referring to ghastly nightmares that she was unable to remember and, at times, also having episodes of sleep-walking.

Georgia came to the consultation with her mother. Georgia was an attractive and intelligent twelve-year-old. She told me about her family and school life. Mrs G was happy to answer my questions or clarify any points about the family life that Georgia was not too sure of. Mrs G looked much younger than her mid-thirties age and she had an easy-going, friendly, and close relationship with Georgia, who was one of three children. Mr G had left the family some years earlier and now lived abroad, but they had kept a close enough relationship that enabled the children to move easily and confidently from one to the other parent. Mrs G held a senior administrative position in a commercial firm and was very involved with the education and general upbringing of her children.

Georgia saw herself as a successful, popular member of her circle of friends and colleagues. Her comments about her parents and other

members of the family seemed reasonable and well balanced. I gradually came to the conclusion that Georgia's nightmares were to be
understood within the context of the attack she had suffered: whatever
unconscious conflicts she might have as a result of previous family
experiences did not seem to have much relevance to the present crisis.

I asked Georgia to tell me the story of the attack in detail. She
answered my questions, but time and again she indicated her puzzlement as to why I insisted she should try to remember the details of
each step she had taken that evening. I explained that the fact that the
nightmares were still haunting her indicated that some element of her
experience that evening must have taken on a particular meaning that
she had not succeeded in working out. She could see the logic of my
words, but several times she tried to dismiss some question either
because she could not remember what happened or because she
thought it could not be important. Fortunately, Mrs G agreed with my
argument, and repeatedly encouraged Georgia to try harder to answer
my questions, which she did.

Georgia and her friend had met other school and neighbourhood
friends at the fair. They had rides in various machines and ate the
usual range of fast foods that youngsters relish at fairs. At one point,
Georgia and her friend decided to have a particular brand of ice cream
and realised they would have to walk a long way to reach the stall that
sold it. They told their friends of their intention and moved away from
the group. As they checked their bearings, they realised that they
could reduce the distance by walking behind some stalls, rather than
along the main walkways. Georgia remembered that they had considered the possibility that there might be danger in taking that shortcut,
but "danger" was used as an umbrella word; they did not discuss
what might be involved.

Georgia told me that as they were walking behind one of the stalls,
they suddenly saw a huge dog lying on the ground. For a moment,
they stood still, thinking what to do and trying to convince themselves
that the dog might remain quiet. But, unexpectedly, the dog took a
short run and jumped on them. Georgia could remember the dog
hitting her and throwing her on the ground, but then there was a
blank and the next datum in her memory was being at home with
mother and sisters, crying.

After some more questions, it was clear that Georgia had told me
everything that she could remember. She had no recollection of her

nightmares, except for those dreams in which the attack was being repeated, but even these would stop precisely at the same point where her recollections stopped. Her mother commented that she had tried many times to help Georgia to remember her movements that evening. As a matter of fact, Georgia's friend had told Georgia and her mother that when both of them began to cry and scream many people had come rushing to find out what had happened. They had helped Georgia to get up and when they saw that she was bleeding, she was taken to the First Aid tent in the fair and, from there, to the Casualty Department of the local hospital. But Georgia knew all this as information given to her, not previously available to her memory.

We had reached an impasse. Considering the age of the girls and the notion of "danger" they had anticipated they might face, it would be conceivable that there was a sexual content to their anxieties. I was, however, loathe to voice such a hypothesis without having some cue that Georgia might recognise as coming from herself. Just to present her with a sexual interpretation "out of nowhere", might lead her to associate this presentation with the experience of the dog jumping on her. I decided, therefore, to try an alternative approach.

I explained to Georgia that sometimes one could reach a lost memory through the use of drawings. Predictably, she looked baffled, suspicious, and embarrassed, but she agreed to give it a try. Normally, in similar consultations, I am careful not to make suggestions to the child, leaving it to them to draw whatever they choose to draw. Here, however, we had a special situation. I had asked endless questions focusing on one single sequence in Georgia's life and I decided, therefore, to depart from my usual technique. I asked Georgia to draw a picture of her meeting the dog.

Georgia's first drawing (Figure 23) shows her together with her friend walking towards the part of the stall where the dog was. I noticed the expression on the dog's face and this did not seem to me particularly fierce (some dog lovers who saw this drawing said that this was a very sensitive picture of a large and lovable dog), but I made no comment. I asked Georgia to draw what happened next.

Her second drawing (Figure 24) shows the dog biting Georgia's lips and drops of blood falling on the ground. Her friend is further back, with an expression of horror on her face. After considering this picture for a while, I asked her to draw what she thought had happened next. She hesitated briefly and drew (Figure 25) herself on

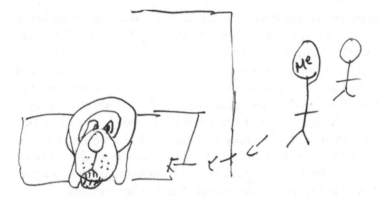

Figure 23.   Georgia's first drawing.

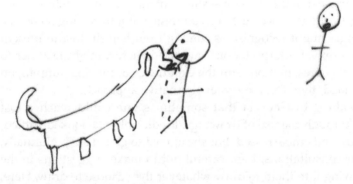

Figure 24.   Georgia's second drawing.

the ground with the dog on top of her, but she decided this was "wrong" and crossed it out. She repeated the same scene a few inches above the wrong image and I noticed that in this picture the dog is entirely beside her body, while in the first one it was placed between her legs, but I said nothing. When I asked what had then happened, she wrote "Blanck" to indicate the gap in her memory, but then went on to draw herself crying and bleeding, already at home, with her mother and siblings staring at her in horror.

By now, I was quite convinced that Georgia had built a sexual fantasy over the attack by the dog, but I had to find a way of conveying this interpretation to her in a manner that might make sense to her. I asked her to go back to the earlier part of her account where she had spoken of "danger". She denied that she had any idea of what kind of

Figure 25.   Georgia's third drawing.

danger she and her friends had in mind. It was impossible to know whether this was a true statement or whether she felt ashamed in front of her mother or myself. A further complication was that she might be trying to guess what answer I wanted from her and, anyway, it was difficult to frame any question without loading it in some direction. Mrs G was following this dialogue without saying anything. I explained my difficulty in wanting to help Georgia to identify what might have been on her mind without influencing her and, finally, mimicking a tone of voice that might sound like her mother's, I said, "Please make sure that you do not move away from your friends! Mind you don't go into dark places and definitely not away from the main paths! You just have to be careful in case you find . . .", and I stopped.

Mrs G smiled. She had now recognised what I had in mind and I think she did give Georgia some cue, because Georgia soon muttered, very quietly, "Some man . . ." Mrs G smiled and confirmed that this was a warning that she issued very forcibly each time Georgia went out with her friends to the park, particularly if there was a fair going on. I asked Georgia what danger men posed, but she kept silent. Mrs G obliged at this point and made explicit that her warnings had included explaining to Georgia about sexual attacks and how to defend herself from this.

I went back to the drawings and called Georgia's attention to her "wrong" drawing. I explained to her my idea of putting two drawings on top of each other, as if they had been made as a single picture. I showed her that I was not just making pictures fit, but that the corners of the pages corresponded to each other. I lifted the superimposed pages (Figure 26) and asked her if she saw anything that struck her as interesting or significant.

Georgia laughed, clearly embarrassed, and said that the dog was now totally on top of her. I explained to her that she *knew* that she had been attacked by a dog that had bitten her lip, but the pictures showed that "deep in her mind" (or words to this effect) she had remembered the warnings about men who could attack her and subject her to a sexual assault, and she had put the two together, so that she was now reacting as if she had been sexually attacked.

Mrs G voiced surprise, but commented, "It makes sense." She was fascinated by my picking up my interpretation from the drawings and asked questions about this. Georgia was visibly relaxed, but looking thoughtful. We agreed to meet again two weeks later, to check on progress.

On the morning of the appointment, Mrs G telephoned the Clinic: Georgia was in bed with 'flu, but she had told the mother that she did not, really, want to see me again. Mrs G added that she was inclined to agree with Georgia, since the nightmares had stopped. Right from the day of our interview, Georgia had slept through the nights and there was, therefore, no reason to see me again. I spotted a thought going through my mind that here they were deciding "to let sleeping dogs lie" . . .

Figure 26.   Georgia's second and third drawings superimposed.

Comment

Nowadays, Georgia would be diagnosed as showing a "post trau-matic stress reaction" and this account shows one way in which such cases can be approached. Follow-up information from the family doctor was that Georgia had not presented further difficulties.

Georgia's history shows how high levels of anxiety produced by a traumatic experience result from unconscious fantasies that are "not allowed" to reach consciousness, let alone be articulated, but find expression in dreams and various symptoms. It is possible that if Georgia could remember and recount the content of her nightmares, then these fantasies might be understood through the analysis of the dreams. Georgia's drawings represent a clear demonstration of how the defence mechanisms that impeded her from recognising and artic-ulating these unconscious fantasies could be by-passed by turning to the language of split drawings.

Paula

Paula had been attending a school for delicate children, but her teach-ers felt that her earlier physical problems no longer justified keeping her out of ordinary school and she was transferred to the local secondary school. Paula found this transition very difficult and began to show signs of distress, which became increasingly severe and, even-tually, she refused to attend school. Mrs P spoke to the teachers, who agreed that Paula should be allowed to return to her former school, but the educational authorities demanded a child psychiatric assess-ment before reversing their decision.

Paula had a long and complex medical history. She started to walk at eighteen months and only spoke when she was four years old. She had frequent attacks of bronchitis, and when she was nine months old a doctor prescribed some codeine mixture and it turned out that Paula was allergic to this: she went into coma and was admitted to hospital. She recovered and was discharged after one week. Another problem area was Paula's weight; she was described as "eating for comfort", and Mrs P told us that after her husband's death, two years previ-ously, Paula had "started to put on 3lb each day, without eating much".

Paula had, apparently, no difficulties attending primary school, but she presented considerable learning problems and required special help, and stayed in primary school for an extra year. That autumn, her father died and "Paula went into a state of shock for some time." Paula was now meant to start secondary school, but, after lengthy discussions, she was given a place at the school for delicate children and Mrs P felt "Paula blossomed there", taking part in all activities and improving her work.

Paula was thirteen years old when seen at the Clinic. Mrs P described her as sensitive, frail, weak, sickly, dependent, miserable, and lacking in confidence; conversely, in their report, the school spoke of Paula as a tall, healthy girl, who preferred the company of boys and enjoyed playing football and cricket.

When we asked about Paula's father, we were told that Mr P had suffered from a gastric ulcer for many years. At one point, his doctors decided he would benefit from surgery and he was admitted to the local general hospital. Unfortunately, one week after returning home from his operation, he had a massive haemorrhage: Paula found him, sitting on the toilet, covered in blood. She had screamed for her mother. When Mrs P came to the bathroom, they thought he was dead, but then they noticed some movement and rushed to call an ambulance that took Mr P to hospital. Mrs P travelled with him in the ambulance; she told us that she offered Paula to join them, but Paula refused this, saying she preferred to go to school. Mr P underwent emergency surgery, but he died a few days later.

Paula was dressed in such a way that when the social worker and I went to the waiting room to meet them, we thought she was a boy. We all went to the social worker's room, where introductions were made and we tried to make Paula and her mother feel welcome. Mrs P soon made it clear that she had only agreed to attend because she saw this interview as the price to pay so as to obtain Paula's transfer to her former school. She did not "believe in discussing the future, since you cannot prevent or change what happens" and, as for the past, "It is best to forget or ignore problems because nothing is gained from thinking about them." For her part, Paula was monosyllabic and unco-operative; when asked about her reasons for not attending her present school, she could only say, "It is too big." After a while, I thought Paula might be more responsive if I saw her on her own, and we moved to another room, leaving Mrs P with the social worker.

Paula appeared, indeed, more relaxed, though she did not seem to find it so easy to articulate her thoughts. Taking it for granted that the episode of her father's haemorrhage would have been a major trauma for her, I asked Paula about this. She told me about finding her father on the toilet, after her mother told her to call him. Paula confirmed her mother's account that she had been asked whether she wanted to accompany them, but Paula said she preferred to go to school; she could not give me an explanation for this choice. She shrugged her shoulders and made a rather painful grimace, but she could not muster any words to justify her decision. When I asked her about subsequent events, she told me that she had never cried when she learnt that her father had died. We went on to talk about her "feeling (she) was a boy"; this had been going on for two years, but again she could give no explanations. I asked Paula whether she thought there was any link between this change and her father's death, but she denied any such connection.

I noticed Paula was looking at some sheets of paper on my desk and I suggested she made a drawing. After some hesitation, she drew a house (Figure 27). I did not make any comment and, after a brief

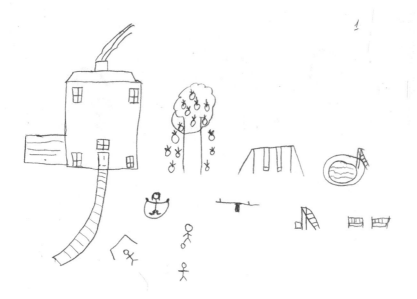

Figure 27.   Paula's first drawing.

pause, she drew a tree, with apples falling from it. I found this a rather unusual picture and asked her about the way in which she had drawn the apples, but Paula could not clarify this, merely shrugging her shoulders and muttering, "I don't know." After a brief pause, she went on to draw the slide, the swing, see-saw, and benches. Much as with the house, I was struck by the barrenness of the picture and I called her attention to this: she could not comment on it. Considering she had drawn these various playground elements, I asked her if she also drew people. She answered that she only did so with "match-stick" images and proceeded to draw the girl with the skipping rope and some boys playing football. "I used to like to be like the girl, but now I prefer to play with the boys," she said.

Here was a spontaneous reference to the question of her gender identity and I was, obviously, interested in this. But, taking into account her difficulties with words, I suggested she might draw these various images of herself. She picked up another page (Figure 28) and drew herself "as [she] used to be"; because "this went wrong", she crossed out this drawing and started another picture (top–middle of page: long hair and skirt), and then drew "how [she] became" (right:

Figure 28.   Paula's second drawing.

long hair and trousers); finally (bottom left: short hair and trousers), "what [she is] like now". Having finished these drawings, Paula waited for my comments. I did think the pictures depicted quite clearly the features that would identify her as "girlish" or, on the contrary, "boyish", but besides acknowledging this fact, I hesitated, not quite certain as to how to proceed. But Paula had left the two pages still glued together and, in line with my previous experience with interviews where children made two sequential drawings, I put the two pictures on top of each other, as if they corresponded to a single mental picture that had been split over two different pages (Figure 29). I lifted the two superimposed pages and held them against the light coming from the window. When Paula saw the falling apples and the girl's face matching each other so perfectly, she said, "She is crying."

I had no doubt in my mind that the tears were a reference to her "never crying" when she found her father and, later, when he died. But I could not just throw this assumption on Paula, as if coming only from my preconceptions. The drawings she had made up to that point did not seem to contain any pointers to the *cause* of the tears and I

Figure 29.   Paula's drawings superimposed.

thought it would be much more useful if we could obtain further clues that might help Paula herself to understand where the tears on the girl's face were coming from. However, because it was so difficult to engage Paula in a dialogue, I suggested we play squiggles. She accepted this and quickly was immersed in the game.

The individual squiggles we made are not reproduced here (they can be seen in *Untying the Knot*, Brafman, 2001, pp. 147–151), but, after a series of drawings, Paula drew the following squiggle (Figure 30). I thought this was a perfect rendering of what she had seen when discovering her father on the toilet, and I proceeded to complete the picture (Figure 31).

Paula showed no surprise at my drawing or at my putting into words that her squiggle gave the essential lines of the picture of her father as she had found him two years earlier. I suggested that his death and the manner in which it had happened had affected Paula very deeply. I said she needed help to work out her feelings about it and that I should see her a few more times, but it was impossible for me to discern how my words were affecting Paula. Her face only showed an expression suggestive of acceptance, but she uttered no words. I offered Paula the opportunity to ask me any questions she might want, but she just shook her head, making a grimace as if to

Figure 30.   Paula's squiggle.

Figure 31.   My drawing on Paula's squiggle.

indicate she had nothing to say. After a pause, I suggested we should rejoin her mother and the social worker.

I told Mrs P that I would be happy to recommend Paula's return to her former school, but I added that I believed that Paula should have some further individual interviews, since I did not think that the school transfer alone would be enough to help her with her problems. Mrs P made it clear that she disagreed with me. She repeated her earlier statement that she was quite convinced that returning to her old school was all that Paula needed to make her again the happy and successful girl she had been. Only reluctantly, did Mrs P agree to a follow-up appointment.

The day before the arranged appointment, Mrs P telephoned the Clinic and told the social worker that Paula had been very upset ever since our meeting and that she had cried most of the day for several days. Paula had told Mrs P that her tears followed our conversation about her father and his death. Mrs P could see no advantage in this and, therefore, she did not wish to expose Paula again to such painful experiences. After much discussion, Mrs P did bring Paula the next day. When I saw Paula on her own, she could not speak much, but she made it clear that it was my talking about her father that had so upset her. However much I tried, Paula was no more forthcoming than she had been at our first meeting.

Though we had no further contact with Paula or her mother, we learnt from the school that soon after the transfer, Paula settled down and became more peaceful and relaxed. It was interesting to hear that since returning to her former school, Paula had approached the school nurse and spent considerable time discussing with her the circumstances of her father's death and her feelings about him—something that she had never done before. For some months, Paula continued to act and dress like a boy, preferring boys' company at playtime, but gradually this subsided, and, by the end of two years, Paula was behaving like other girls in her class.

Comments

Paula's split drawings and her last squiggle are perhaps the most dramatic examples I have found of what I consider to be the language of drawings. Finding her father covered in blood had proved to be a severe traumatic experience. She had not been able to cry or to speak about her pain, and the various problems that eventually brought her to the Clinic were the indicators of the underlying conflicts. But only when Paula was drawing did her unconscious manage to find the split images that would convey the nature of her repressed pain. The fruits falling from the tree that then became Paula's tears must have opened the way for her to draw on paper the main lines of the picture that so shocked her: her father sitting on the toilet. Paula could now be conscious of her pain and embark on her mourning—and, correspondingly, free herself of the various symptoms she had been presenting.

Sonia

This twelve-year-old girl was referred because of her compulsion to cut herself, but it soon emerged that her family also found it very difficult to cope with her defiant and sometimes bizarre behaviour. Sonia's mother and an older sister came to the diagnostic consultation, but a younger sister refused to attend. Sonia restricted herself to keeping a smile on her face—mother and sister defined this as her typical attitude of defiance and mockery. I wondered if it also expressed embarrassment, but I ended up believing it signalled a message of detachment from people and subjects being discussed.

The family history was extremely complex. Sonia's father had died some six years earlier, but their accounts of past and present life suggested he was still a live presence in the family. Considering the children, there were arguments regarding which personality and behaviour traits had been inherited from which parent. Episodes of earlier years were recounted in order to emphasise the importance of Mr S to the dynamics of family life. One of these referred to Sonia accidentally cutting herself and being assisted by her father: apparently, a conversation had ensued where Sonia asked him if he was not afraid of blood and, supposedly, her father responded that, in fact, he liked the sight of blood.

Because Sonia seemed so reluctant to engage in a discussion, I suggested she might make a drawing. She drew (Figure 32) a man on a horse, but said she did not know whom this was meant to represent. Her sister, however, commented that their father loved horses. I

Figure 32.   Sonia's first drawing.

voiced some puzzlement about the features of the horse-rider, and Sonia explained that she did not know how to draw people, tending to depict them as stick figures, and proceeded to draw several of these at the bottom of the page. Somehow, she decided to draw her father and went on to draw him lying sideways on the top of the page. After some minutes, I suggested she made another drawing, and Sonia took another sheet of paper, on which she drew (Figure 33) two horses standing side by side and a cat a little distance from them. She then added a poster on which she wrote "Wild Ponies", presumably establishing this was the territory inhabited by the two ponies she had previously drawn. I decided to superimpose the two drawings (Figure 34) and Sonia, as much as her sister and Mrs S, was surprised to recognise the pinpointing of Mr S as the symbol of the identity of the ponies. It was quite clear that Sonia did not see herself as one of the "wild ponies", that is, one of the S children. Whatever lay behind such an idea, it was obvious that all recognised that she had been Mr S's favourite child and a surprising piece of evidence for such a belief was put forward: he had hit Mrs S and the other girls many times, but never had he hit Sonia.

The family was seen again, and Sonia's self-cutting did abate and eventually stopped.

Figure 33. Sonia's second drawing.

Figure 34. Sonia's drawings superimposed.

Comment

Seeing how the superimposed pictures showed Sonia as the cat and not one of the ponies, I wondered whether this meant she did not truly see herself as one of the S family. But I had to take on board the fact that they immediately found a different explanation for Sonia being different to her siblings—she was described as the one Mr S treated with special kindness.

As far as I know, this was the only situation where Sonia seemed to indicate her belief of being different to her siblings, but I did not feel able to pursue such a possibility. If Sonia was being seen in individual therapy, this could certainly be investigated.

Two sides of the same sheet of paper

The following pictures show the same phenomenon of two drawings, each with a clear, definite meaning of its own, suddenly acquiring a new meaning when seen together, as if each one complemented the other. Because they are drawn on two sides of the same sheet of paper, the question arises that the artist might have aimed, quite deliberately, at obtaining that effect: that is, as if the second picture corrected or completed the meaning of the first one. Having watched the drawings being made, I am convinced that this was not the case. Furthermore, most of the papers on which the drawings were produced were not so transparent. But, more important, the separate drawings corresponded to different views that the child had on the particular matter being illustrated, while the final image, resulting from seeing the split images united, was so significant in making sense of the person's conflicts.

Anne

Anne was thirteen years old when she was referred for a child psychiatric assessment of her problems. Over the preceding months, she had presented a series of physical symptoms and a dramatic change in her general mood and her attitude to her parents. At school, the teachers had also introduced changes in her daily schedule so as to help Anne to cope with her physical complaints and frequent anxiety crises.

Anne had two older siblings who lived away from home and the parents had a warm, close relationship. Her mother had devoted her life to looking after the family and her father was an active sportsman, who had gradually become a coach of professional and amateur sportsmen. However, just over one year before our interview, Mr A had developed a severe form of arthritic illness that made it impossible for him to continue with the work he loved.

Seen on her own, Anne was an intelligent and articulate teenager, well able to describe her conflicts with peers and the difficulties she found at home. When seen together with one or both parents, Anne was a different person: introverted, tense, and clearly watchful of what she might say.

In my initial interview with Anne, I found her most co-operative, but somehow I could not feel that I had learnt what exactly worried her. She described difficulties with falling asleep, trouble with appetite, a feeling of failing to deal with her parents in the same amicable, respectful way she had always maintained, but all this was too composed, not quite allowing me to grasp what anxieties she was struggling with. I decided we should play squiggles, hoping this might give me a better understanding of what tormented Anne.

Anne was clearly a gifted artist. Only two of the pictures made in our squiggle game are reproduced here. Anne's first drawing (Figure 35) shows how she turned my squiggle into a horse that is pretending to eat grass, but in fact is watching what goes on around him. Anne's second drawing (Figure 36) represents what she called "after the pride comes the fall", and this was meant to represent how her father had changed from a first-class sportsman into a sad, grumpy, debilitated, arthritic victim who was all the time finding fault in what Anne did or said.

In another interview, two weeks later, Anne drew her fish tank (Figure 37). She was quiet, looking rather desolately at her drawing. "They move slowly . . . it's very soothing . . ." After a pause, she told me about two male goldfish she had some time back—they had both died. "There must be something about male goldfish . . .

Figure 35. Anne's first drawing.

Figure 36. Anne's second drawing.

SILVER AND GOLDIE MY GOLDFISH

Figure 37.   Anne's fish tank.

perhaps they are weaker . . ." It was rather difficult to engage in a conversation and I asked her if she wanted to make another drawing. "I don't mind . . ." She went on to tear the page from the pad and turned it over, going on to draw (Figure 38) Heaven, Earth, and Hell on the other side. Earth shows "our graveyard", Heaven has the angels, and the spots represent souls. Hell has only the Devil, because "people would have burned up anyway . . ." Somehow, she added two lamps, "the only light there". I lifted the page and suggested she should look at the pictures against the light (Figure 39). She smiled, "the goldfish are watching the devil . . ." I asked her whether it was possible that when she watched "the soothing fish tank" she found herself thinking about death and the Devil. She smiled and said, "I suppose so . . ." She went on to express some of her concerns over her father's state of health and growing physical and emotional incapacitation.

We saw Anne and her parents for several interviews and they reported continuous, sustained improvement. The psychologist who had originally been called in by the school to help with Anne's problems also reported that Anne had made considerable progress at school and was now virtually "the old Anne we knew", attending her classes normally.

Figure 38.   "Heaven, Earth, and Hell".

Comment

However painful the confrontations with her father, it was clear that Anne was unable to voice her concerns over his health. Presumably, her "fighting father" could still be seen as strong, but the problem was that the "fighting Anne" felt hurt, weak, and terrified that her father might die. It is difficult for any child in any family to voice such anxieties, but in her drawings Anne managed to express what worried her and kept her awake for hours in bed.

I believe Anne's drawings should also be seen as "split images", even if it might be more difficult to explain the superimposition of the images. When the drawings are split on two separate pages, we can hypothesise the brain retaining the same boundaries of the area where the images are displayed, while, in Anne's case, this formulation would not be applicable, unless we postulate a similar "brain manoeuvre" that ensured the superimposition of the relevant elements of the original split images.

Figure 39.   Joined up images.

Alan

Alan was fifteen years old when his stepmother contacted the Clinic to ask for help. She felt he was unhappy, difficult to contact, apparently obsessed with religion and totally disinterested in his school and social activities, except for music, an activity to which he devoted quite a good part of his free time. She also felt that Alan was "all the time" clashing with his father over a wide range of matters. When the Clinic's educational psychologist contacted Alan's school, they reported him as sensible, smart, and studious, but often appearing "vacant".

Alan had a traumatic childhood. His mother had left the home when he was four years old and he moved to his paternal grandparents' home. His father remarried when he was seven years old and his grandfather, to whom he was very attached, died not long afterwards. He moved to his father's new home, where he met two older step-siblings. His relationship with his stepmother was reasonably good, but there were occasional clashes that tended to lead to his father's intervention and consequent times when Alan felt alone and rejected. By the time he came to see us, he had developed a great interest in the local church—not only did he take an active part in their musical activities, but he had become very friendly with the vicar and his young and attractive wife. Both his parents resented this interest of Alan's and put considerable pressure on him to move away from the church and the couple who ran it.

Alan was happy to see me and answered my questions without any difficulty. He recounted his history and spoke about his interests and activities, being rather careful with his words only when speaking about father and stepmother. He did have memories of his mother's presence in his life, but he believed she had died: this was a subject he had never raised with his father.

As Alan had mentioned that he enjoyed drawing, I asked if he wanted to make a picture. He took a small piece of paper and carefully drew (Figure 40) a woman seen sideways, sitting on a chair: he said this was the vicar's wife, but he could not explain why he had drawn her in that position. He drew a tomb, which I assumed was a

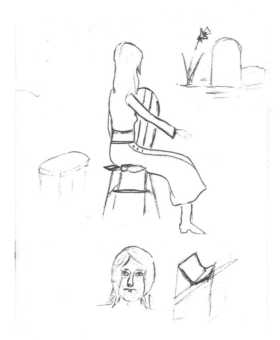

Figure 40. Alan's first drawing.

reference to his belief that his mother had died. He drew Paul McCartney (very popular in those days!) and a letter M, which he could not explain. We talked about these pictures for some minutes and I asked him if he wanted to make another drawing. Saying "yes", he turned the piece of paper over and proceeded to draw on the other side of the page (Figure 41).

Alan drew an altar, which he said was the one at the church he frequented. When I picked up the sheet of paper, I suddenly saw (Figure 42) how woman and altar fitted together. I showed this to Alan—he was very surprised and smiled, rather embarrassed. Considering what he had said about his mother and how attached he was to the vicar's wife, I suggested that perhaps unconsciously this kind woman had taken his mother's place, hence his valuing so much the time spent with her and in the church. Alan said this was quite a likely possibility.

I suggested Alan should have individual psychotherapy and he was happy to take this up. He did make good progress and was able to lead a more enjoyable life at school and with his friends. Unfor-

Figure 41.   Alan's second drawing.

Figure 42.   Alan's joined-up drawings.

tunately, this did not happen at home, where clashes with his parents continued to occur.

Comment

Slow, careful consideration of Alan's relationship to his parents and the growing importance that the church carers had acquired in his life would sooner or later lead to the realisation that the vicar and his wife had taken on the role of ideal parents. His choosing to draw the vicar's wife was a pointer to the special role that she had acquired in his unconscious, but Alan would never formulate explicitly such a sentiment in thoughts or words. However, using the language of images and splitting the fundamental elements of his unconscious fantasy into two separate drawings, Alan could express his unconscious feelings.

From a pragmatic, clinical point of view, Alan could recognise the understanding of his unconscious feelings as originating from his own graphic images and not as an inference put forward by the professional he was consulting.

Jessica

The referral letter from the general practitioner painted a dramatic picture of Jessica's problems: "This nine-year-old girl has been suffering with a phobia of dead bodies—she is paranoid of death. She is having nightmares and goes into a state of anxiety with hyperventilation. She does well at school and has no problems there. She has loving parents and there is no family history of a psychiatric nature or any question of abuse to the child. I gather this child follows her mother everywhere, sits in the kitchen and stays near the toilet if her mother is inside. She thinks she is going to die."

I saw Jessica and her mother together. A friendly, warm, smiling couple, they made themselves quickly at home. Mrs J apologised that her husband had had a last minute commitment and had been unable to attend. Jessica was a healthy, articulate nine-year-old, self-possessed and confident. She said she liked her school, she had many friends, and was well liked by her teachers. She enjoyed telling me that she was among the best pupils in her class.

Jessica told me of her fear that she herself or someone else might die. She found it puzzling that this never happened outside their home, or when she was playing or concentrating on something, "I guess that having fun keeps the fear away!" she said with a smile. But from time to time, she becomes aware of a sense of gripping terror and she will run to her parents, throw herself on the ground, cry with painful, loud sobs, bang her head violently against the wall, run wildly around the house; one or both parents will try to quieten her down, but they "know by now that nothing helps". Apparently, the crises come to an end with Jessica falling asleep, out of sheer exhaustion.

I asked Jessica when these attacks had started. She said "about two years ago" without hesitation, but she was unable to pinpoint any event that might have marked the beginning of the crises. Mrs J confirmed her daughter's assertion that no event of particular significance had taken place at that point of time. About the frequency of the attacks, Jessica answered, "At the beginning, they came on about once each month, but then they became more frequent and, recently, they may come even every week." But she also had nightmares. She recounted that, whatever the dream was about, at some point a multitude of ghosts appear and descend on her, trying to kill her. "I just lie there, on the bed, very scared, but waiting to fall asleep." Mrs J corrected her, saying that for many weeks now when Jessica cries during the night, her father calls her and she has been "sleeping across the bottom" of the parents' bed. Jessica looked embarrassed, but confirmed her mother was right.

Having heard the story of "the problems" and coming to the conclusion that I could not find what else to ask Jessica about the circumstances surrounding these events, I invited Jessica to make a drawing, while I would talk to her mother. We were sitting round quite a small table, so that both Mrs J and I could see what Jessica was drawing. She made some vertical lines at the bottom of a page (Figure 43), looking

Figure 43. Jessica's first drawing.

like a garden fence, but soon she turned the page over and started another picture (Figure 44). From the way she handled the crayons and paper, it was clear that she was well accustomed to depicting what ideas she wanted to put on paper. She was following the conversation, frequently making comments and engaging in some dialogue.

I asked Mrs J to give me some idea of herself and the family. She had lived in the vicinity of the Clinic for many years and had many friends in the local community. She was proud of her home and of the success her children achieved at school.

I was told that Mr J was also in his early thirties. He worked as a plumber and came from a large family. The wider family was in good health and nobody suffered from the kind of fear that affected Jessica. Here, Jessica butted in to say, with an impish smile, that her father was very scared of the dentist and so was Mrs J herself. Mrs J laughed, and explained that she had told Jessica about being frightened of the dentist in order to reassure her that everyone had something they were scared of.

Figure 44. Jessica's second drawing.

I asked Mrs J about her parents, and she said her father had died some years earlier and her mother had remarried soon afterwards. She explained that her parents had separated many years before her father's death. I asked how her father had died. Mrs J sobered up and her voice changed its tone. One day, he was visiting the Js and he had fallen down the stairs in the house, hitting his head on the banisters. He had not sought medical attention, but he developed "a bump" that soon turned sceptic and he died in a matter of days. The atmosphere in the room had changed. From a very rosy picture of life, I was now told that the paternal grandmother had long been a diabetic, and "about two years ago" she suffered a fall and hit her head on the ground. Soon afterwards she suffered the first of what had now become three strokes. Curiously, there was nothing in the voices of either mother or daughter to indicate that they had noticed that both grandparents had hurt their heads with serious consequences. A very heavy silence followed. Mrs J clearly did not know how to continue and Jessica was suddenly as if frozen, staring at her drawing. I imagined she had heard these accounts many times before and I wondered how she would react to these references to "hitting the head". I asked her if it was because of these accidents that she *hit her head against the wall*. Mrs J barely had time to show her surprise, because Jessica immediately nodded her head and said "yes".

Mrs J said she just did not believe Jessica's answer. Jessica told her mother that she often looked up her grandfather's pictures. Mrs J pointed out that there was only one, a rather poor photo taken not long before his death. But Jessica reminded her that grandfather was also part of a picture taken at her wedding—"Oh, that one? I had forgotten it . . ."

After a pause, I asked about Mr J's family. Besides his mother's strokes, there were no illnesses here, but dramatic stories followed. His father had always been a very violent man. After several traumatic experiences, Jessica was no longer allowed to visit the grandparents' house, though occasionally some arrangements were made for her to meet the grandmother on some neutral ground.

It was not difficult to correlate Jessica's fears and her obsession with death and loss with the illnesses of her grandparents, but what to make of the stories about violence? Both mother and child were now silent and I did not know what further questions to ask, so I turned to the picture Jessica had made. This was a beautiful and colourful house, with a brilliant sun in the corner of the page and a bright blue representing the sky that enveloped the house. Jessica confirmed that this was a picture of her own house and described what exists behind each window—she was puzzled by my questions, but she still answered them. I was trying to obtain her private idea of what life they led and how she represented this. When I asked her about the lines on the other side of the page, she said she had "wanted to draw something, but it went wrong". I indicated I had my own idea of what the lines represented, but I asked Mrs J what she made of them. She had no idea and Jessica told us that she had started to make a gate, which would be at the corner of the house. She challenged me to say what I had made of it and I admitted that I had first thought it was a fence, but after hearing of what happened to her grandfather I now thought it might be the banisters of some staircase. Jessica laughed, "Oh, no! Just a fence!"

Again we had a pause. Mrs J looked quite different. She was thoughtful and, taking a deep breath, she told me that her husband had been involved with the authorities not only because of conflicts with his father, but also due to some offences related to his work. I learnt that, not very long before our meeting, the police had called at the house and had taken Mr J away in handcuffs. I felt it would not be appropriate to ask for many details.

Following my experience with drawings made on both sides of the page, I lifted the sheet of paper and asked Jessica whether she noticed anything in particular (Figure 45). She noticed the superimposition of the sun and the "fence": she burst out laughing, "It's *inside the fence!*" It was perhaps not necessary, but I still said that the sun was *behind bars* and Jessica laughed at this image that she could recognise as apposite.

We could now discuss how both Jessica and her mother were afraid of losing Mr J. If Jessica's problems had started with unconscious fantasies related to damage to the head that could cause illness and death, her present phobic behaviour and nightmares were linked to her fear of losing her father and her need to share her anxieties with those of her mother's. As happens so often at such points in an interview Jessica was nodding and looking quite relieved, while Mrs J seemed to think that this was all too far-fetched. She asked the classical "but what CAN I do?", and I suggested she should spend some

Figure 45. Jessica's joined-up drawings.

time with Jessica every night, discussing whatever Jessica wanted to raise.

When I next saw Jessica and Mrs J, Jessica told me that she felt better, "firm", she said, and Mrs J confirmed that Jessica had not "thrown any more wobblies". When I spoke to the GP after a couple of months, I was told that Mrs J had not made any further reference to the earlier difficulties with Jessica.

Comment

Of course, it is possible that the superimposition of sun and fence is no more than a coincidence, but it was certainly an accurate image of Jessica's fear of her father being imprisoned by the police: an anxiety that she had not previously formulated in words. Splitting the image of the happy family house from the dreaded situation of having her father taken away enabled Jessica to let Mrs J know exactly what led her to cling to her parents and so often seek to ensure they remained alive and available.

Robert

The beautiful split image created by Robert came in a session of a long-term individual psychotherapy. This was a young man of twenty-two years of age who sought therapy for a series of problems linked to his social and sexual life. He had found employment after finishing his secondary education and it is difficult to understand his not pursuing an artistic career when he was clearly a very gifted artist.

It was not in every session that Robert decided to draw, but this was a means of communication that he tended to turn to when finding it difficult to decide what exactly to speak about. In this specific drawing, he depicted his leaving home and finding his way to the Clinic where he saw his therapist. On one side of the sheet of paper (Figure 46), he drew his being "squashed" against a wall by a friend

Figure 46.   Robert's first drawing.

and then his attempting to get on a bus, only to be pushed off by the conductor. Instead of picking up another sheet of paper, he turned that sheet over and drew (Figure 47) his arriving at the Clinic, being met by his therapist, who takes him to her room and they settle down to his session—he is now happy, relaxed and ready for his session.

It is then quite fascinating to find that when the sheet of paper is held against the light (Figure 48 and the enlarged portion shown in Figure 49), the conductor and the therapist are completely superimposed, and instead of welcoming him, the therapist is now pushing him off! Coincidence? Or is this his unconscious anxiety that behind her professional façade, the therapist is, actually, wishing he were not there?

Figure 47.   Robert's second drawing.

Figure 48.   Robert's drawings.

Figure 49.   Enlarged image of corner of Robert's drawings.

Enclosed images

R eading Freud's books led me to see his work on Leonardo da Vinci (1910c), where he put forward an analysis of what he considered to be a disguised image of a bird that could be detected in a classical painting of Leonardo's. Clearly, this would constitute an expression of an idea of which the artist was unconscious. However, I had also seen other works of art where this enclosed image could be found. If, in some cases, this final image rendered elements from the artist's unconscious, I also found pictures where the artist displayed these "enclosed images" as an artistic artifice. Salvador Dali has produced several pieces with this ingenious artefact (see, for example, "Slave Market with the Disappearing Bust of Voltaire", 1940, Plate 1, used by permission of The Salvador Dali Museum, St Petersburg, Florida, USA). It is possible that it was my familiarity with these works that enabled me to spot an example of the use of this particular "language" when seeing the picture made by a young patient during a consultation.

Plate 1.   Slave Market with the Disappearing Bust of Voltaire (1940). Oil on canvas (8¼ × 25⅜ inches. © Salvador Dalí. Fundación Gala-Salvador Dalí (Artist Rights Society), 2011. Collection of the Salvador Dalí Museum, Inc., St Petersburg, FL, 2011.

Rachel

This eleven-year-old girl was referred to the Clinic by her GP. She had been complaining of various physical symptoms that often prevented her from attending school, and also of night terrors. The GP had referred Rachel to a gastroenterologist, but all tests proved negative. He had also counselled Rachel and her parents about various ways in which they might deal with bedtime routines, so as to reduce Rachel's level of anxiety, but this had failed to produce results. He decided to explore emotional factors, and referred Rachel to a clinical psychologist. Because no significant progress occurred after several weeks, the parents returned to the GP and, after further discussion, the GP recommended a psychiatric assessment.

Both parents brought Rachel to the diagnostic interview. Father was a salesman at a local shop and Mrs R devoted herself to looking after the home and her two children. They described their family histories and this seemed very normal. Marriage was harmonious and

Rachel's younger brother was developing normally. Both children attended a local school and were described as "high average" in their performance. Rachel made herself at home without any trouble. She told me of her multiple physical symptoms and how she regretted missing school because of her pains. The sleep disturbances led to a general feeling of weakness the following day, but Rachel stressed how hard she tried not to give in to the desire to lie down and sleep.

As we discussed Rachel's progress, it emerged that these difficulties had started soon after a holiday, when the family had gone to a camping site where they had spent several earlier holidays. This time, however, unexpected problems had occurred. Apparently, one of the families staying at the site had clashed with other holidaymakers and violent fights had taken place. The R family were not involved, but both their children had been intensely upset by being so close to the noises and the threat of escalating confrontations. As it happens, Rachel's brother was perturbed for a few days, but then seemed to overcome the trauma.

Rachel had been joining in with what her parents said and telling me details of some of the above events. I decided to ask her to make a drawing. She asked me, "A drawing of what?", but I just answered that she should feel free to draw anything she wanted. She went on to make a very elaborate drawing (Figure 50), showing a housing estate and depicting a girl standing by a swing and a slide, while another girl was playing near a garden. The various paths linking the houses and blocks of flats were drawn in detail and a man was shown coming down one of these passages. Rachel was able to describe all these details in a flowing account, but she denied any particular significance of the various features of the drawing.

Somehow, I thought that the lines linking the houses on the right and those at top centre seemed to delineate the figure of an animal. I put this to Rachel, but she could not see anything of the sort. I put another sheet of paper on her drawing and traced what I believed were the contours of an animal (Figure 51). Rachel's face lit up: she now had a broad smile and promptly embarked on an account of her nightmares, where monsters threatened to attack her, and she explained that they looked like the animal–monster of the tracing.

Both parents and I were taken aback—not only by my "seeing" the monster, but by the unexpected enthusiastic reaction of Rachel. As she gradually came to a stop, the parents asked me how we should

Figure 50.   Rachel's drawing.

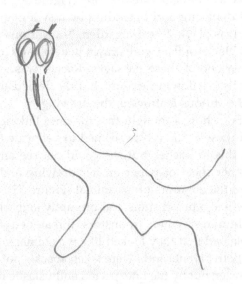

Figure 51.   My tracing of the "animal" in Rachel's drawing.

Figure 52.   Rachel's drawing and my tracing superimposed.

proceed. Did I think Rachel required further interviews? I did believe that this might be advisable, but I chose to tell them that we should observe how Rachel progressed over the next few weeks and we could then meet again and discuss how to proceed.

When I saw the family again, I learnt that Rachel had not had any further nightmares, but she still struggled with various anxieties related to her relationship with peers. I recommended that she should see the Clinic's child psychotherapist, and she did have a period of regular therapy.

Art colleges

Many years ago, I attempted to carry out an experimental study to check whether this split images phenomenon would occur in other than a clinical situation. It soon became clear that my ability as a research worker did not reach the required standards that might give credibility to my findings. Nevertheless, I did see instances where split images were clearly present. What was the level of incidence? A very important question, but I cannot offer a proper answer. I visited art college classes, each with different numbers of students who volunteered to take part in my experiment. In one group, I found four "positive" cases out of thirteen students, while in another class of twelve students I found one case where an image had been clearly split into two.

When I met the group of students, I told them of my work with children and adolescents, emphasising my interest in pictures, but not making explicit the actual reason for my approaching them. I take it for granted that my introducing myself as a psychoanalyst and a child and adolescent psychiatrist must have had a special meaning to most, if not all, students. Those were times when being "a shrink" still produced a strong impact on people, and one had to assume that those students were aware of seeing one of these in

front of them and not another artist or a research psychologist, speci-
alities that were "less threatening", less loaded with particular preconceptions of "danger". Introducing oneself as an analyst nowadays,
we no longer hear "An analyst? Oh, I must watch what I say!" that
was so common years ago. Perhaps a proper research project should
involve a more "neutral" person, but, at the time, I felt I had to give
a proper introduction of who I was and what work I was involved
in. But even after taking this factor into consideration, it is still
difficult to establish precisely how this information affected each
student.

Having introduced myself, I asked the group to draw whatever subject they wanted and the only definite stipulation I made
was that they should make at least two drawings. When they finished their drawings, each student brought the pictures to me and
described what they had drawn. Some had put their names on the
paper, others had not. Some wrote explanatory words, others did
not. As they told me what the pictures meant, I made brief notes on
a piece of paper. I expressed my thanks to each student and to the
group as a whole, but I never made any comment about specific
pictures.

As with the other cases described earlier, I do see these split
pictures as the result of an unconscious process and not a simple coincidence. But, in the following examples, I cannot offer any evidence
other than the drawings themselves, since I did not ask the students
for any complementary data they attached to the pictures they had
drawn.

John

In John's first drawing (Figure 53), we see a man peacefully sitting
under an apple tree. Apparently, he is sleeping and has a contented
smile on his face, unaware that an apple is falling on his head. John
turned to another page and we now (Figure 54) have another man
shooting an arrow that hits the apple and pins it on the trunk of the
tree, thereby saving the sleeping man from being hit by that apple. If,
however, we examine the two pictures superimposed together (Figure
55) the arrow is hitting the man's head!

Figure 53. John's first drawing.

Figure 54. John's second drawing.

Figure 55. John's drawings superimposed.

Christina

On the first page, we see a dog chasing a rabbit and eventually catching and eating it (Figure 56). Then, on the next page, the dog is sleeping peacefully. As Christina numbered the pictures, the sleeping dog is "number 6", that is, resting after eating the rabbit (Figure 57). But superimposing both pages (Figure 58), it would seem that the sleeping dog is actually dreaming the whole chase, an interpretation that might be supported by the fact that picture number 5 shows the dog eating from his "normal" eating tray. Furthermore, this might explain the artist's choosing to place "drawing 2" above the image of rabbits running in the field as "drawing 1". An alternative explanation might be that the sleeping dog is remembering his earlier chase, but either way it is interesting to note the superimposition of the running and the sleeping images of the dog.

Figure 56.   Christina's first drawing.

Figure 57.   Christina's second drawing.

Figure 58.   Christina's pictures superimposed.

Monica

Monica drew an experience she had while travelling in an Eastern country. She and a friend had only managed to find seats in the "lower class" compartment of the train (Figure 59) and they are depicted (her friend reading a book and Monica looking out of the window) when trying to "escape" from the noise and dirt of the wagon. In the next picture (Figure 60), two prostitutes arrive and start to make approaches to two male passengers. A third picture (Figure 61) shows Monica telling off the prostitutes, telling them to behave themselves, and respect the people on the train. If we superimpose pictures 2 and 3 (Figure 62), it is quite striking how both prostitutes are seen precisely

Figure 59.   Monica's first drawing.

Figure 60.   Monica's second drawing.

S

Figure 61.   Monica's third drawing.

Figure 62.   Monica's second and third drawings superimposed.

in the same position. But superimposing pictures 1 and 2 (Figure 63) or 1 and 3 (Figure 64), it is Monica's friend who is now seen in the position of one of the prostitutes: is there any unconscious idea in Monica's mind that somehow sees her friend as a prostitute? Even

Figure 63.   Monica's first and second drawings superimposed.

Figure 64.   Monica's first and third drawings superimposed.

more puzzling is then to note that in the superimpositions of 1 and 2, as well as in 2 and 3, Monica is seen "taking the place" of the man that the prostitutes are addressing.

Thomas

This art student told me that he remembered something a friend's child had told him and this led him to draw three pictures that he named as the story of "the last tree in the world". The first has on the near side a large tree with owls sitting peacefully on its branches, and on the other side of a gorge we can see a large number of trees (Figure 65). The second drawing (Figure 66) depicts a man chopping a large number of trees, and, finally, the third picture (Figure 67) shows a large number of stumps, while across the gorge we can see the "last tree in the world", suitably meriting the visit of a long queue of people.

If the concept of split pictures is accepted, what are we to make of the clear, precise superimposition of the man and the "last tree in the world" (Figure 68)? Supposedly, this image might suggest a self-

Figure 65. "The Last Tree in the World"—1.

Figure 66.   "The Last Tree in the World"—2.

Figure 67.   "The Last Tree in the World"—3.

damaging thought or, alternatively, an idea of becoming the sole survivor of meaningful losses, but the context in which these drawings were made did not allow for any investigation of how the artist himself would react to this finding.

Figure 68. Thomas's first and second drawings superimposed.

Summing up

The subject of "communications" has always fascinated me. Being brought up in a family where three languages were often used, I soon learnt the mystery of uttered words that were not meant to be understood, while the tone of voice employed would at times lead one to guesses that were difficult to confirm or to ignore. Still a child, I found that the choice of a piece of music to be played on an instrument or on a recording was a strong pointer to the mood of the person involved. Next came the discovery that tics involved more than the mechanics of body parts. But the most precious finding was in a humorist's dictum that "communication is what the other hears". This wise and most perceptive joke highlighted the difficulty that affects so many of our social interactions: how can we be certain that our words were correctly understood? How can we be sure that we have truly understood what someone wanted to convey to us?

In the context of ordinary social life, with luck, we have the emotional atmosphere that allows us to check and clarify any doubts that interfere with the flow of the conversation. But if a person is struggling with feelings that involve pain or anxiety, then we find a complex network of difficulties affecting that person's capacity to express what torments him. Whatever the person's age, very often he has no access to the words that might convey his internal conflicts. People interacting with that person might believe he is deliberately refusing to express what affects him, but it is certainly true that most times this is not the case. The child complaining of nightmares might not be aware that these follow fears of a parent threatening to leave the family, much as an adult experiencing abdominal pains might not immediately link these with the news of a friend being taken ill. And yet, here are examples of how these people's bodies come to express the emotional conflicts that the person is experiencing.

When dealing with children, these difficulties are even more acute. But it is very many years ago that it was found that children often expressed in their drawings elements of the conflicts they were experiencing. Knowing of this, psychoanalysts who worked with children made sure that their patients could use the appropriate materials to employ other means of giving expression to their experiences of themselves and the world in which they lived. And I followed this practice in my work—not only with children and adolescents, but, at times, also with adults.

And one day I discovered that single drawings could, at times, represent only a part of an underlying emotional experience that "completed" its expression in another picture drawn after that first one. At first, I thought this was no more than a coincidence, but time came to show me that this was a "strategy" similar to what we find in ordinary verbal language. Drawings clearly constitute a language of their own, and I believe this finding deserved proper further investigation. This is the reason for the publication of this book. As a clinical tool, I hope my findings will help colleagues in their work. Research work should give closer and more detailed understanding of this splitting mechanism, so well known in actual words, but apparently not previously described in drawings.

REFERENCES

Arnheim, R. (1969). *Visual Thinking*. Berkeley, CA: University of California Press.

Brafman, A. H. (2001). *Untying the Knot: Working with Children and Parents*. London: Karnac.

Brafman, A. H. (2004). *Can You Help Me?* London: Karnac.

Di Leo, J. H. (1973). *Children's Drawings as Diagnostic Aids*. New York: Brunner/Mazel.

Freud, A. (1927). Introduction to the technique of child analysis. In: *The Psycho-Analytical Treatment of Children*. New York: International Universities Press, 1959.

Freud, S. (1910c). *Leonardo Da Vinci and a Memory of his Childhood. S.E., 11*: 57–138. London: Hogarth.

Freud, S. (1923b). *The Ego and the Id. S.E., 19*: 3–66. London: Hogarth.

Johnson, M. K. (1985). The origin of memories. In: P. C. Kendall (Ed.), *Advances in Cognitive Behavioral Research and Therapy*, Volume 4 (pp. 1–27). New York: Academic Press.

Kellogg, R. (1969). *Analyzing Children's Art*. Palo Alto, CA: Mayfield.

Klein, M. (1932). *The Psycho-Analysis of Children*. London: Hogarth, 1960.

Laplanche, J., & Pontalis, J.-B. (1973). *The Language of Psycho-Analysis*. London: Hogarth.

Lowenfeld, V. (1947). *Creative and Mental Growth*. New York: Macmillan, 1978.

Luquet, G.-H. (2001). *Children's Drawings (Le Dessin enfantin)*. London: Free Association Books.

Moore, M. S. (1994). Reflections of self: the use of drawings in the evaluation and treatment of children with physical illness. In: D. Judd & A. Erskine (Eds.), *The Imaginative Body* (pp. 113–144). London: Whurr.

Perelberg, R. J. (2007). Space and time in psychoanalytic listening. *International Journal of Psychoanalysis, 88*: 1473–1490.

Piaget, J., & Inhelder, B. (1967). *The Child's Conception of Space*. New York: W. W. Norton.

Stern, W. (1924). *Psychology of Early Childhood*. New York: H. Holt.

Winnicott, D. W. (1960). Ego distortion in terms of true and false self. In: *The Maturational Processes and the Facilitating Environment*. London: Karnac, 1990.

Winnicott, D. W. (1971). *Therapeutic Consultations in Child Psychiatry*. London: International Library of Psycho-Analysis.

INDEX